Patcha Bhujanga Rao
Patcha Preethi

Employee Absenteeism in Organizations

Patcha Bhujanga Rao
Patcha Preethi

Employee Absenteeism in Organizations

LAP LAMBERT Academic Publishing

Impressum / Imprint

Bibliografische Information der Deutschen Nationalbibliothek: Die Deutsche Nationalbibliothek verzeichnet diese Publikation in der Deutschen Nationalbibliografie; detaillierte bibliografische Daten sind im Internet über http://dnb.d-nb.de abrufbar.
Alle in diesem Buch genannten Marken und Produktnamen unterliegen warenzeichen-, marken- oder patentrechtlichem Schutz bzw. sind Warenzeichen oder eingetragene Warenzeichen der jeweiligen Inhaber. Die Wiedergabe von Marken, Produktnamen, Gebrauchsnamen, Handelsnamen, Warenbezeichnungen u.s.w. in diesem Werk berechtigt auch ohne besondere Kennzeichnung nicht zu der Annahme, dass solche Namen im Sinne der Warenzeichen- und Markenschutzgesetzgebung als frei zu betrachten wären und daher von jedermann benutzt werden dürften.

Bibliographic information published by the Deutsche Nationalbibliothek: The Deutsche Nationalbibliothek lists this publication in the Deutsche Nationalbibliografie; detailed bibliographic data are available in the Internet at http://dnb.d-nb.de.
Any brand names and product names mentioned in this book are subject to trademark, brand or patent protection and are trademarks or registered trademarks of their respective holders. The use of brand names, product names, common names, trade names, product descriptions etc. even without a particular marking in this works is in no way to be construed to mean that such names may be regarded as unrestricted in respect of trademark and brand protection legislation and could thus be used by anyone.

Coverbild / Cover image: www.ingimage.com

Verlag / Publisher:
LAP LAMBERT Academic Publishing
ist ein Imprint der / is a trademark of
AV Akademikerverlag GmbH & Co. KG
Heinrich-Böcking-Str. 6-8, 66121 Saarbrücken, Deutschland / Germany
Email: info@lap-publishing.com

Herstellung: siehe letzte Seite /
Printed at: see last page
ISBN: 978-3-659-46231-3

CONTENTS

LIST OF TABLES
LIST OF FIGURES

CHAPTER NR.	PARTICULARS	PAGE NR.
CHAPTER- 1	INTRODUCTORY	06 - 20
CHAPTER- 2	CONCEPTUAL STUDY ON EMPLOYEE ABSENTEEISM	21 - 50
CHAPTER- 3	INDUSTRY PROFILE AND PROFILE OF RMM FOOD PRODUCTS PRIVATE LIMITED	51 - 74
CHAPTER- 4	EMPIRICAL STUDY ON EMPLOYEE ABSENTEEISM	75 - 100
CHAPTER- 5	SUMMARY OF FINDINGS, SUGGESTIONS AND CONCLUSIONS	101 - 104
	BIBLIOGRAPHY	105 - 108
APPENDIX	QUESTIONNAIRE	109 - 110

LIST OF TABLES

TABLE NR.	PARTICULARS	PAGE NR.
TABLE 3.1	Country-wise export of mangoes from India during 2001-02	57
TABLE 3.2	State-wise growing belts	59
TABLE 4.1	Opinion of employees' absence due to unexpected work	75
TABLE 4.2	Opinion of employees regarding getting absent to the employment due to health	76
TABLE 4.3	Opinion of employees in taking leave without permission	77
TABLE 4.4	Opinion of employees on compensation for the work they perform	78
TABLE 4.5	Employee opinion on the working environment in the organisation	79
TABLE 4.6	Opinion of employees on their relationship with supervisor	80
TABLE 4.7	Opinion of employees on satisfaction and co-worker relationship	81
TABLE 4.8	Employees opinion on satisfaction towards grievance handling procedure	82
TABLE 4.9	Employees opinion on job satisfaction	83
TABLE 4.10	Employees opinion on bad working conditions resulting in absenteeism	84
TABLE 4.11	Employees opinion on heavy work load causing absenteeism	85
TABLE 4.12	Employees opinion on safety measures provided by the organization	86
TABLE 4.13	Employees opinion on other sources of income	87
TABLE 4.14	Employees opinion on shift allotment duty by the management	88
TABLE 4.15	Employees opinion on number of working members in the family	89

TABLE 4.16	Employees opinion on reaching factory late resulting to absenteeism	90
TABLE 4.17	Employees opinion regarding arrival to the factory	91
TABLE 4.18	Employees opinion on their bad habits causing absenteeism	92
TABLE 4.19	Employees opinion on the extra health and hygienic benefits	93
TABLE 4.20	Employees opinion on health problems leading to absenteeism	94
TABLE 4.21	Opinion of employees on the welfare facilities provided by the organization	95
TABLE 4.22	Employees opinion on absenteeism with regard to designation	96
TABLE 4.23	Employees opinion on absenteeism with regard to sex	97
TABLE 4.24	Employees opinion on absenteeism with regard to age	98
TABLE 4.25	Employees opinion on absenteeism with regard to qualification	99
TABLE 4.26	Employees opinion on absenteeism with regard to service	100

LIST OF FIGURES

FIGURE NR.	PARTICULARS	PAGE NOS
FIGURE 3.1	Organization structure	72
FIGURE 3.2	Office on special concerns	73
FIGURE 4.1	Graphical representation of opinion of employees' absence due to unexpected work	75
FIGURE 4.2	Graphical representation of the opinion of employees regarding getting absent to the employment due to health	76
FIGURE 4.3	Graphical representation of the opinion of employees in taking leave without permission	77
FIGURE 4.4	Graphical representation of the opinion of employees on compensation for the work they perform	78
FIGURE 4.5	Graphical representation of employee opinion on the working environment in the organization	79
FIGURE 4.6	Graphical representation of the opinion of employees on their relationship with supervisor	80
FIGURE 4.7	Graphical representation of the opinion of employees on satisfaction and co-worker relationship	81
FIGURE 4.8	Graphical representation of employees opinion on satisfaction towards grievance handling procedure	82
FIGURE 4.9	Graphical representation of employees opinion on job satisfaction	83
FIGURE 4.10	Graphical representation of employees opinion on bad working conditions resulting in absenteeism	84
FIGURE 4.11	Graphical representation of employees opinion on heavy work load causing absenteeism	85
FIGURE 4.12	Graphical representation of employees opinion on safety measures provided by the organization	86
FIGURE 4.13	Graphical representation of employees opinion on other sources of income	87

FIGURE 4.14	Graphical representation of employees opinion on shift allotment duty by the management	88
FIGURE 4.15	Graphical representation of employees opinion on number of working members in the family	89
FIGURE 4.16	Graphical representation of employees opinion on reaching factory late resulting to absenteeism	90
FIGURE 4.17	Graphical representation of employees opinion regarding arrival to the factory	91
FIGURE 4.18	Graphical representation of employees opinion on their bad habits causing absenteeism	92
FIGURE 4.19	Graphical representation of employees opinion on the extra health and hygienic benefits	93
FIGURE 4.20	Graphical representation of the employees opinion on health problems leading to absenteeism	94
FIGURE 4.21	Graphical representation of the opinion of employees on the welfare facilities provided by the organization	95

PROBLEM AFFIRMATION

Employee presence at work place during scheduled time is highly essential for the smooth running of production process in particular and the organization in general, despite the significance of employee presence, employee sometime fail to report at work place during scheduled time, which is known as absenteeism. Absenteeism at the operative level is a crucial problem in industries.

The study of absenteeism is very important because excessive absenteeism tells upon the productivity of organization during periods when the production is at peak and skilled labor is scarce, the absence of employees will be very much disruptive to production and morale. Excessive absence involves a considerable loss to the organization because work schedule are upset and delayed, the management has to give the overtime wages to meet the delivery dates.

Thus, it is necessary to determine its extent and causes to minimize the absenteeism. To facilitate this, proper investigation should be made from every department in the organization for various causes of absenteeism by such division as age, sex, days of the week and classes of job.

Hence, the need for investigation into absenteeism has become a dire need rather than academic interest. As such, the present study is undertaken to minimize the absenteeism concentrating on the attributes such as sickness, accidents, poor control, lack of interest and attitude

OBJECTIVES AND PURPOSE OF THE STUDY

1. To identify the reasons for absenteeism of employees in RMM Food Products Private Limited.

2. To assess the reasons for absenteeism and its impact on work and working environment in RMM Food Products Private Limited.

3. To review the variables that reduces the rate of absenteeism and suggest measures to minimize absenteeism in RMM Food Products Private Limited.

REVIEW OF LITERATURE

A person who is habitual absentee worker is called chronic absentee worker the 50 cases classified in to 5 following categories entrepreneur, status seeker, epicureans, and family oriented, sick and old. Some of the causes are as fallowed job factor, environmental factors.

Entrepreneur: This class of absenteeism that their jobs are very small for their total interest and personal goals. They engage themselves in other social and economic activities to fulfill their goals.

The status seeker: This type of absenteeism enjoys or perceived a higher ascribed social status and is keen on maintaining it.

The epicureans: This class of absenteeism does not like to take up the jobs, which demand, initiative responsibility discipline and discomfort. They wish to have the money, power status, but are unwilling to work for their achievement.

Family oriented: This type of absenteeism often identified with the family oriented activities

Sick and Old: This category of absenteeism is mostly unhealthy weak constitution (or) old people[1].

---

[1]Mirza saiyadin (1988), Tata Mc GrawHill Publications, 3rd edition, New Delhi, pp. 421-425.

The employer is responsible for designating an absence or leave as FMLA leave on basis of information provided by the employee. Employers can require workers to provide medical certification of such series illness and can require a second medical opinion employers can also exempt from FMLA key salaries employed who are among their highest employers must maintain health insurance benefit and give workers their highest employers must maintain health insurance benefits and give the workers their previous job jobs when their leaves apartment of labor.

Nevertheless the law still covers 300,00employers and 45million employees in the private sector, and about 15 million more in state and local government.

This completes the discussion of "absolute prohibition" against discrimination. The following section discusses non discrimination as a basis for eligibility for the federal funds. Employee may dread coming to work because co-worker are unpleasant, the job has become unchallenging they are piercing conflicting demands from job and family or the supervision[2].

The problem of poor attendance includes Absenteeism / tardiness. Poor attendance can became a serious problem that leads to discharge for just cause. If poor attendance are forced to increased their efforts to compensate for people who shrink their responsibilities.

Sometimes employee are absent or tardy for legitimate reason example sickness, childcare Problems , inclement , weather , or religious beliefs .managers should identify those employees who have legitimate reasons

---

[2] Wayne F. Cascio (1986), Tata Mc Graw Hill Publications, 6th Edition, New Delhi, pp 91-92.

- 8 -

and threats the differently than they treat those who are chronically absent or tardy .

When discipline an employee for poor attendance, manager need to consider several factors managers should be aware of patterns of poor attendance within a work unit. Systematic absenteeism or tardiness may be symptom of job avoidance. Employee may dread coming to work because co-worker are unpleasant, the job has become unchallenging they are piercing conflicting demands from job and family (or) the supervision is poor. A disciplinary approach is not the best way to deal with this type of absenteeism. It would be better for the manager (or) company to look for ways to change the work environment possible solutions to job avoidance are designing jobs or, when the problem is widespread, restricting the organization.

Causes of absenteeism:
1. Serious accidents
2. Low morale.
3. Lack of Job satisfaction
4. Boredom of the job
5. Poor working conditions
6. Transportation problems
7. Stress
8. Lack of satisfaction from present work.
9. Poor welfare facilities[3].

While an employer may find that the overall absenteeism rate and cost are within an acceptable range, it is still advisable to study the statistics to determine whether there are patterns in the data. Rarely does absenteeism

---

[3] David B .Balkin (2001) , Prentice-Hall Pvt., Ltd., 3rd Edition, New Delhi, pp477-478

spread itself evenly across an organization. It is very likely that employees in one area may have nearly perfect attendance records, while others in a different area may be absent frequently[4].

The following are general causes of absenteeism.

Maladjustment with the working conditions:
If the working conditions of the company are poor, the workers cannot themselves with the companies' working condition.

Social and religious ceremonies:
Social and religious function diverts worker attention from the work

Unsatisfactory housing conditions:
This is caused at work place.

Poor welfare facilities, unhealthy working conditions
Absenteeism among workers in our factories in the manufacturing sector in most part of India has been for a major problem for a long time .In its extreme from as many as40%(or) more workers may not present themselves for work in a particular shift (or) in a particular day in a particular department, causing the severe disruption of production schedules .Low output in one department then has a chain reaction down the line.

The monthly average for the whole factory would however between 10%to35percent the peaks varying from factory to factory. Considerable research on absenteeism has taken place in the western countries and the primary theme highlighted is that the problem is caused by the prevailing climate at the workplace.

---

[4]George Bohalander and Vienna Vera (2010),1st Edition, Engage Learning India Pvt., Ltd, Australia, pp.97-100

They also switched onto incentives for better attendance .In the 1992, encashment of leave was introduced and in mid 1996 the cash attendance incentive on monthly basis came in a part of an overall settlement with the union.

In our country the faith in cause and effect relationship tends to be rather weak, and   thus the search for root cause is not persevered. In shows that those employees who have low job satisfaction   tend to be absent .The connection is not always sharp, for   a couple of reasons, first, some absences are caused by legitimate   medical reasons therefore a satisfied necessarily plan to be absent ,but they to be find it easier to respond to the opportunities to do so .These voluntary absences often occur with frequency a certain cluster of employee and usually occur on Mondays   or Fridays. Where involuntary (medically related) absenteeism can sometimes be predicated (e.g. for surgery) and often be reduced through the use of record checks ,different approaches are needed for absences caused by poor attitudes.

Some employee place all of an employee occurred time off into paid leave bank of useable days (also known as paid time off). Vacation time, sick leave, holidays, personal days all enter the bank, and the employee can use them for any reason. This approach gives the employee can use them for any reason .This approach gives the employee greater control over when to take days off ,and the employer gains greater predictability of those occasion, other employers have successfully used incentives to control absenteeism[5].

Absenteeism is a universal problem in industry and is not peculiar to Indian industries. But the rate of absenteeism has been relatively higher in India.

---

[5] V.K Sharma (2002), VIVA Books Pvt., Ltd., New Delhi, Mumbai, pp.125-127.

1. The rate of absenteeism has been more than 10 percent.
2. A small percentage of employees account for a large percentage of the total absenteeism. This chromic absenteeism has negative perception and attitude.
3. Absenteeism has been greater in night shifts than in day shifts.
4. Absenteeism has been greater higher in the department. Where supervisor work oriented and careless for employee welfare
5. Women tend to be absent more frequently than supervisor and manager.
6. Absenteeism is generally higher in large organization than in small organization
7. Absenteeism is lowest on the pay day and in highest immediately after the payday[6].

By absenteeism we mean a condition that rises when employee fails to come the to work when he is scheduled to work. The study of absenteeism is very important because excessive absenteeism tells upon the productivity of organization .during periods, when the production is at a peak and skilled labor is scarce, the absence of some employee will be very much disruptive to production and morale. Excessive absent involves a considerable loss to the organization because work schedule are upset and delayed, the management has to give the overtime wages to meet the delivery dates.

To minimize the absenteeism, it is necessary to determine its extent and causes. To facilitate this, proper records should be kept by every department for various causes of absenteeism by such division as age, sex, days of the week and classes of job. Generally the following reasons are considered for absenteeism at work.

---

[6] Gupta (1996), Sultan Chand and sons, 9th edition, New Delhi, pp.321-333.

Sickness: Sickness is high on the list of the causes of absenteeism, running high as 50% of absenteeism.

Accidents: Industrial accidents occupational diseases bring about absenteeism depending upon the nature of process are called accidents.

Poor control: Poor production and material control can result in absenteeism unless the flow of work between the deport is balanced and continuous, workers may stay away from their jobs because they lose their interest in the work and also lose the feeling of the importance of being dependable.

Lack of interest: Lack of interest and lack of feeling or responsibility and worth. Wholeness is also the fundamental causes of absenteeism.

Attitude: Attitude of mind, caused by environmental and sociological factors may condition some to develop a feeling or irresponsibility about going to work.

Some of generalization: Women are absent more often than men; Operative employees are absent more frequently than their supervisors[7].
Employee absenteeism is one of the major management problems faced by most of the organization, today. Absenteeism has many varies implication of business organization, in which the main direct and indirect influence economic[8].

Absenteeism at the operative level is a crucial problem in some industries absenteeism is unauthorized absences from work place. According wasters

---

[7] Rakish k. Choprav (1989), First and Second edition, Kitab Mahal, Allahabad, pp.380-381.
[8] Ushers,(2010), Journal of Business Management, Christ university,pp.11-13

"absenteeism is the practice or a habit of being an absenteeism and an absentee is one who is habitually stays away".

Labor Bureau, shiplap has defined absenteeism as "the failure of the worker to report for work when he is scheduled to work". A worker is to be considered as scheduled to work when the employer has work available for him the worker is aware of it" .However , for identifying the magnitude of both authorized and unauthorized absence is taken into consideration, and absenteeism is expressed as follows.

Absenteeism = NUMBER OF MAN DAYS LOST DUE TO ABSENCE/ NUMBER OF MAN DAYS SCHEDULED TO WORK *100

Factors of Absenteeism:
There are contrasting views on the causes of absenteeism .According to the one school of thought, absenteeism is due to the part of workers .The worker in the process of early stages of industrialization is more prone to absenteeism prolonged and sporadic withdrawal from industrial work
Absenteeism is due to the factors that influence a workers commitment it is grouped into three categories.

Organizational factor:
There are various organizational factors which cause work alimentation resulting into absenteeism. In research study following organizational factors has been found responsible.

In some industries where work is monotonous, the rate of absenteeism is high.

Leniency towards absenteeism causes high rate of absenteeism.

Environmental factor:

Various factors of the country particularly in the socio-economic factors and religious cultural factors are responsible for high rate of absenteeism various environment factors of the country cause high absenteeism in following ways.

Socio-economic factor:

1. Due to migratory nature of labor force in India, workers do not develop emotional belongingness with their work places.
2. Workers generally live in UN hygienic and poor conditions.
3. Workers generally have more number of dependent children, coupled with unhygienic living condition they face the problem of sickness quite frequently which results in absenteeism.

Religious and cultural factor: India population consists of multi-religious and cultural factors with each group having its own religious festivals, customs and traditions[9].

Absenteeism among workers in our factories in the manufacturing sector in most part of India has been for a major problem for a long time .In its extreme from as many as40%(or) more workers may not present themselves for work in a particular shift (or) in a particular day in a particular department, causing the severe disruption of production schedules .Low output in one department then has a chain reaction down the line.

The monthly average for the whole factory would however between 10%to35percent the peaks varying from factory to factory. Considerable research on absenteeism has taken place in the western countries and the

---

[9] L.M. Prasad (2007), Sultan Chand & Sons, 2nd Edition, New Delhi, pp. 683-685.

primary theme highlighted is that the problem is caused by the prevailing climate at the workplace.

They also switched onto incentives for better attendance .In the 1992, encashment of leave was introduced and in mid 1996 the cash attendance incentive on monthly basis came in a part of an overall settlement with the union.

In our country the faith in cause and effect relationship tends to be rather weak, and   thus the search for root cause is not persevered. In shows that those employees who have low   job satisfaction tend to be absent .The connection is not always sharp, for a couple of reasons ,   first, some absences are caused by legitimate   medical reasons therefore a satisfied necessarily plan   to be absent ,but they to be find it easier to respond to the opportunities to do so .These voluntary absences often occur with frequency a certain cluster of employee and usually occur on Mondays   or Fridays .Where involuntary (medically related) absenteeism can sometimes be predicated (e.g. for surgery) and often be reduced through the use of record checks ,different approaches are needed for absences caused by poor attitudes.

Some employee place all of an employee occurred time off into paid leave bank of useable days (also known as paid time off). Vacation time, sick leave, holidays, personal days all enter the bank, and the employee can use them for any reason. This approach gives the employee can use them for any reason. This approach gives the employee greater control over when to take days off ,and the employer gains greater predictability of those occasion ,other employers have successfully used incentives to control absenteeism[10].

---

[10] V.K Sharma (2002), VIVA books Pvt., Ltd., New Delhi, pp.125-127.

HYPOTHESES OF THE STUDY

1. There is no significant difference of opinion between superior and subordinate employees with regard to the attributes that result in absenteeism among employees in RMM Food Products Private Limited.

2. There is no significant difference of opinion between male and female employees with regard to the attributes that result in absenteeism among employees in RMM Food Products Private Limited.

3. There is no significant difference of opinion between below 40 years and above 40 years of age with regard to the attributes that result in absenteeism among employees in RMM Food Products Private Limited.

4. There is no significant difference of opinion between 0-10 years, 10-20 years and above 20 years of service with regard to the attributes that result in absenteeism among employees in RMM Food Products Private Limited.

DATA COLLECTION

PRIMARY SOURCES

Responses collected with the help of the questionnaire administered to the employees and management of; is the main primary source of data for this research work. The primary data are collected in three phases.

In the first phase, the purpose and objectives of study are explained to them and requested to go through the schedule thoroughly.

In the second phase doubts of the respondents about the contents of the schedule, if any are clarified.

In the third phase, the filled in schedules are collected from the respondents by holding further discussions to elicit additional information.

SECONDARY SOURCES

The secondary sources of data are collected from the magazines, journals, bulletins, web sites and annual reports, etc., published by the organization.

In addition to these, several structured interviews, and unstructured interviews, have also been conducted with experts on the subject and also a number of persons who are connected in one way or other, either directly or indirectly to know about absenteeism.

SAMPLE FRAME

The sample size was put to 120 chosen from various functional areas of the organization. The departments are first divided into strata and thus simple random sampling has been followed to select employees.

TOOLS FOR DATA COLLECTION

The questionnaire with a set of questions was constructed and administered to the sample of employees to elicit first hand information relating to the role, implementation, and perceptions of employees with regard to the absenteeism in RMM Food Products Private Limited.

TOOLS FOR ANALYSIS

The interview schedule method is used for gathering data, which are relevant for the study conducted among various categories of employees RMM Food Products Private Limited. The data collected through the schedules from primary sources have been processed and the results are analyzed by applying appropriate statistical tools.

SCOPE OF THE STUDY

The research covers a major organization. This organization is well known for the best performance. Therefore, to lend a comprehensive study to this research work at RMM Food Products Private Limited, was chosen. The effectiveness of absenteeism in RMM Food Products Private Limited, is examined.

LIMITATIONS OF THE STUDY

The questionnaire used for the purpose of collecting the opinions of employees has the following limitations.

1. Certain terms used for the purpose of the study are new to the respondents as they are not in general use.
2. In the process of data collection some of the respondents have expressed difficulty in answering the schedule.
3. The present study is confined to a sample of employees RMM Food Products Private Limited.

PLAN OF ANALYSIS

The data collected through the schedule have been processed in tune with the objectives set and the results are tested with hypotheses formulated by employing appropriate statistical tools.

FIELD STUDY

The field investigation will be conducted in the month of May 2013 by adopting personal interview method. During the course of study considerable help has been received from employees of RMM Food Products Private Limited.

PLAN OF THE STUDY

The plan of study is as follows

Chapter-I Introduction, deals with research methodology and design of the present inquiry.

Chapter-II Conceptual study on aspects of absenteeism.

Chapter-III deals with industrial profile and company profile

Chapter-IV Empirical study of on absenteeism in RMM Food Products Private Limited.

The **final chapter (Chapter-V)** presents summary of findings and conclusions.

INTRODUCTION

Absenteeism is a habitual pattern of absence from a duty or obligation. Traditionally, absenteeism has been viewed as an indicator of poor individual performance, as well as a breach of an implicit contract between employee and employer; it was seen as a management problem, and framed in economic or quasi-economic terms. More recent scholarship seeks to understand absenteeism as an indicator of psychological, medical, or social adjustment to work.

High absenteeism in the workplace may be indicative of poor morale, but absences can also be caused by workplace hazards or sick building syndrome. Many employers use statistics such as the Bradford factor that do not distinguish between genuine illness and absence for inappropriate reasons.

As a result, many employees feel obliged to come to work while ill, and transmit communicable diseases to their co-workers. This leads to even greater absenteeism and reduced productivity among other workers who try to work while ill. Work forces often excuse absenteeism caused by medical reasons if the worker supplies a doctor's note or other form of documentation. Sometimes, people choose not to show up for work and do not call in advance, which businesses may find to be unprofessional and inconsiderate.

This is called a "no call, no show". According to Nelson & Quick (2008) people who are dissatisfied with their jobs are absent more frequently. They went on to say that the type of dissatisfaction that most often leads employees to miss work is dissatisfaction with the work itself.

The psychological model that discusses this is the "withdrawal model", which assumes that absenteeism represents individual withdrawal from dissatisfying working conditions. This finds empirical support in a negative association between absence and job satisfaction, especially satisfaction with the work itself. Medical based understanding of absenteeism find support in research that links absenteeism with smoking, problem drinking, low back pain, and migraines. Absence ascribed to medical causes is often still, at least in part, voluntary. Research shows that over one trillion dollars is lost annually due to productivity shortages as a result of medical-related absenteeism, and that increased focus on preventative wellness could reduce these costs.[3] The line between psychological and medical causation is blurry, given that there are positive links between both work stress and depression and absenteeism.[2] Depressive tendencies may lie behind some of the absence ascribed to poor physical health, as with adoption of a "culturally approved sick role". This places the adjective "sickness" before the word "absence", and carries a burden of more proof than is usually offered.

Evidence indicates that absence is generally viewed as "mildly deviant workplace behavior". For example, people tend to hold negative stereotypes of absentees, under report their own absenteeism, and believe their own attendance record is better than that of their peers. Negative attributions about absence then bring about three outcomes: the behavior is open to social control, sensitive to social context, and is a potential source of workplace conflict.

Thomas suggests that there tends to be a higher level of stress with people who work with or interact with a narcissist, which in turn increases absenteeism and staff turnover.

THE 5 CAUSES OF EMPLOYEE ABSENTEEISM AT THE WORKPLACE

Finding out the causes of absenteeism of employees and why they take unplanned leaves.

What is defined as "absenteeism"? According to online dictionaries, it is "frequent or habitual absence from work". It occurs when an employee takes both planned and unplanned leaves. But it is the latter that causes much problem for employers throughout the world. Ask any employer and they will tell you that their definition of absenteeism is a decrease in productivity. Look deeper and you will realize that this will mean that organizations will need to incur additional costs and time to find and train replacements to perform the absentee's work. In fact, employee's unplanned absenteeism is by far one of the most problematic faced by most organizations.

ROOT CAUSE OF ABSENTEEISM

1. Employee's Attitude

This is probably the main cause of misused absenteeism at the workplace. An employee's work attitude will provide hints on the level of commitment he or she has towards their work. If employees have good work attitude, they will not take leaves unless necessary and they will plan their leaves well in advance so that proper delegation of duties can be arranged before that. On the other hand, should the employee have poor work attitude, then chances are they will misuse leaves entitlements and may even have other issues like discipline and integrity.

2. Length of Employment

Surveys have shown that the longer the employee is attached to the organization, the lesser unplanned leaves taken, though there are exceptional cases. This is most likely due to the fact that organizations would have gotten rid of employees who indulged in absenteeism much earlier in their career.

Also, level of position too plays an important factor with the more senior employees being less likely to log in many missing workdays. In short, it is usually the junior employees and the new hires who tend to take unplanned leaves.

3. Work Pressure

Naturally, it goes without saying that when the work pressure goes up, absenteeism rate too will go up. Sometimes, employees in trying to avoid stressful situations e.g. difficult meetings would coincidently report in "sick "or having "family commitments" on that day. It is obviously an excuse to take the day off in order not to face such pressures.

4. Relationship with Superiors

What are the working relationships like in the office? Are the heads of department putting too much pressure on their staff or are the managers demanding beyond what was expected from their subordinates? In recent surveys, it was a surprise that a high number of employees cite "poor relationship with superiors" as the main reason why they choose to stay away from work. Employees, especially junior positions would rather not report to work in a bid to avoid confrontation with their demanding bosses or as an act of defiance.

5. Job Satisfaction

Other than to earn a salary, the other pulling factor why people seek employment is because of job satisfaction. This is also the reason why people change jobs or work environment. Some employees prefer doing the same thing over and over again and will not seek new responsibilities, while others find it boring to perform monotonous functions. But in both cases, absenteeism will occur when their level of satisfaction is lower than what they would accept in their daily work.

It is therefore extremely important to have absenteeism tracked and under controlled and in order to do this; employers must address the needs of their employees. Employees are not to be treated as slaves and at the same time, leaves are not to be abused. There should be mutual respect between both parties in order to have a workable solution.

ABSENTEEISM IN THE WORKPLACE

Handling absenteeism at the workplace is tricky and challenging for the management. Dealing with it requires a certain degree of control and tact from the management's side. This article delves deeper into the causes of absenteeism and lists a few ways to control it.

Habitual or chronic absence from work or other regular duties is defined as 'absenteeism'. In most cases, it is an acceptable reason for breach of contract between the employer and the employee, since it violates the basic clause of the employee's obligation to complete the assigned duties.

From the management's point of view, absenteeism needs to be handled with a certain measure of consideration, depending upon the reasons causing it. In fact, the causes of absenteeism decide the course of action to be followed.

1. **Culpable absenteeism** is when the employee skips work and fails to give a reasonable justification for having done so.

2. **Non-culpable absenteeism** is when the employee skips work due to justified reasons (ill health, injury, etc.).

Culpable Absenteeism

On the surface, culpable absenteeism can be likened to committing professional suicide. But it remains so only at the surface level. To take stringent action against an employee without investigating the reasons behind it can amount to negligence as well. Listed here are some possible reasons behind culpable absenteeism.

1. Lack of Interest in Work

Everyone needs a reason or a motivating factor to come to work. For some, it may be the money; for the moneyed ones, it could be the stimulating work environment; still others could have varied reasons. Whatever it may be, the lack of a motivating factor can be disillusioning enough for someone not to report to work, amounting to culpable absenteeism.

2. Disputes/Harassment at the Workplace

Disputes at work can be a source of great distress for anyone. If the constant bickering begins to intrude on to the person's productivity, reporting to work won't be seen as a viable option by him/her. Also, any form of bullying or sexual harassment can lead to culpable absenteeism if the employee, for reasons best known to him/her, chooses to stay away from work, rather than report it.

3. Attitude Problems

The devil-may-care attitude has ruined a lot of careers, and by all means, is an unpardonable offense. It is incorrect to assume that this problem is solely found in the younger lot of employees. Senior workers who begin to think of themselves as indispensable have also been known to skip work without providing reasons.

How is Culpable Absenteeism Handled?

When an employee takes an extended period of absence, or takes intermittent leaves from work, without any justified reason, the management has to seek an explanation for the same. In case the employee fails to provide answers, disciplinary action could be initiated by the company.

The nature of the disciplinary action will firstly depend on the company rulebook. Other factors like the employee's behavioral history, overall performance, previous achievements or reprimands (if any), duration of service, current circumstances, and the severity of the offense need to be taken into account. The company comes to a decision after analyzing these conditions, which may or may not result in termination of employment.

Non-culpable Absenteeism

Non-culpable absenteeism is the toughest to manage, and to contain. The simplest way chosen by companies is to have a set of rules to be followed regarding permissible leave of absence. To be effective, these rules are to be conveyed to each employee, along with the consequences of refuting them. Rules regarding attendance must be reinforced, and slackness in this area should receive reprimands.

Non-culpable absenteeism can be a result of an illness, or an injury, or any grave issue that is communicated to the company by the employee. It is the company policy that dictates how each case should be considered.

How is Non-culpable Absenteeism Handled?

Communicate with the employee, with a view to understand the reason behind his/her absence. Reasons involving illnesses or injuries are justified, and need to be supported by medical documents. Other reasons caused by personal problems should be dealt with sensitivity, and the outcome should result from healthy discussions.

Absenteeism caused by health problems or disability should be carefully handled. Any waivers in attendance rules should be based on the medical reports provided by the employee, and opinions from healthcare professionals.

It is the company's duty to ensure that the employees are given a healthy environment to work in. In case of any work-related hazards, precautions and safety measures must be in place. The company should not, in any manner, contribute to absenteeism by providing work conditions that are below par and dangerous.

360° EFFECTS OF ABSENTEEISM:

- The employee loses income, and incurs additional expenditure on whatever caused the absence like sickness, travel or celebrations
- The employer incurs loss of work hours, sick pay, overtime or payroll plus training costs of temporary staff and attrition costs as well as costs in lowered productivity, quality and output with a possible loss of customers. There will be additional administrative costs with the rescheduling and hiring efforts, and some end up over-staffing at additional cost.

- Colleagues suffer stress brought on by the additional load of work and deadline pressures along with a feeling of demoralization and/or victimization.

- The Government incurs higher costs in social security payments.

CAUSES OF ABSENTEEISM

- Employee's personal reasons/agenda, sickness/accidental injuries, family problems, substance abuse, poor fitness
- Work place issues like harassment, bullying, stress, communication breakdown or high workload
- Unhappiness with work environment
- Boredom on the job and low morale
- Lack of leadership and poor quality of supervision
- Availability of income protection and other benefits
- Sick building syndrome; or unhealthy working conditions like inadequate ventilation, exposure to volatile chemical or air-borne biological contaminants from indoor or outdoor sources could cause ill-health amongst one's employees.

SEVEN STEPS TO MANAGING ABSENCE IN THE WORKPLACE

To tackle absenteeism effectively, says Paul Roberts, you must establish a solution that lets you detect and address the situation early to avoid short-term absenteeism becoming a long term issue.

1. Ensure you have a clear policy in place

Your company policy should be easy to understand and not open to varying interpretations. It should outline details such as when an employee is entitled to be absent from the workplace, at what time the employee must inform their line manager that they are absent, and where employees should go for support.

2. Act on day one

The first action to manage absenteeism should be on the first day that an employee is not present in the workplace. Check the facts surrounding the absence and address any resulting workload issues to ensure business continues. Line managers should highlight the services available to support the employee such as health insurance policies, company doctor services or an employee assistance programme. Ensure your line managers are fully supported and have the relevant training to ensure they keep within the employment legal framework, such as the Disability and Discrimination Act (DDA), Medical Reports Act and the Data Protection Act.

3. Review at week three

This trigger point is to catch cases that start to become long-term. Fifteen days of absence is nearly twice the national average. A system that highlights an employee who is absent for 15 days will ensure that the organisation is supporting the employee, their family, and facilitating return to work.

Discussions should focus positively on when the employee is likely to return. If the case is serious, occupational health professionals can be utilised to give an independent medical opinion. Managers can base their business decisions on this information and take it into account if the DDA applies.

4. Monitor trends

Trends often emerge among absent employees. Working practices, times of opening and commercial deadlines can all play a part, rather than illness itself. Ensuring you record reasons for absence will enable you to identify trends in the workplace to help avoid future absentee cases.

5. Nominate departmental responsibility

Integrating health services is the key to providing the best and fastest support to the employee, resulting in an early return to work. In many organisations, a range of departments have some input into health services, such as compensation and benefits, health and safety, and HR. Often, these services overlap, leading to duplication. Nominate one department to be responsible for all health providers, insurers and services, to achieve economies of scale and to avoid duplication.

6. Involve others

Absence management is a team effort and should not fall to just one person. Involving relevant parties in the solution will relieve the burden and highlight that tackling absenteeism is a normal part of working at your organisation, and not a flash-in-the-pan project.

7. Communicate

Make sure all employees know what support is available and how to access it.

THE RESPONSIBILITIES OF THE SUPERVISOR

In addition to ensuring that work is appropriately covered during the employee's absence, there are a number of other critical actions that supervisors need to take to manage absenteeism. They should:

1. Ensure that all employees are fully aware of the organization's policies and procedures for dealing with absence,
2. Be the first point of contact when an employee phones in sick,

3. Maintain appropriately detailed, accurate, and up-to-date absence records for their staff, (e.g., date, nature of illness/reason for absence, expected return to work date, doctor's certification if necessary),
4. Identify any patterns or trends of absences which cause concern,
5. Conduct return-to-work interviews, and
6. Implement disciplinary procedures where necessary.

THE RETURN-TO-WORK INTERVIEW

The training of supervisors in how to best manage absenteeism should include instruction on how to conduct effective and fair return-to-work interviews. Recent national surveys indicate that these interviews are regarded as one of the most effective tools for managing short-term absenteeism.

The return-to-work discussion will enable the supervisor to welcome the employee back to work, in addition to demonstrating management's strong commitment to controlling and managing absenteeism in the workplace. The interview will enable a check to be made that the employee is well enough to return to work.

The goal is to foster an open and supportive culture. The procedures are in place to make sure that help and advice is offered when needed and to ensure that the employee is fit to return to work. Employees will usually appreciate the opportunity to explain genuine reasons for absence within a formalized structure. Should the supervisor doubt the authenticity of the reasons given for absence, he/she should use this opportunity to express any doubts or concerns.

The supervisor should then brief the returning employee about the current situation (i.e., what tasks are now priorities, what work has already been carried out and where the employee should now focus his/her efforts).

At no point during the meeting should the interview become a form of "punishment," but should be seen as an occasion to highlight and explain the repercussions of absence within the department. The vast majority of employees derive a sense of pride and achievement from their work and management should be encouraged to treat these individuals as responsible adults.

Most employees understand reasonable rules and do not want to be threatened into compliance. The small percentage of employees who indeed have an absence problem will require close supervision and possibly even punitive measures for excessive absenteeism. These few employees who are irresponsible should be handled individually and firmly.

The following guidelines outline the recommended steps to be taken in cases where short-term absence is considered to be above an acceptable level in a particular period of time.

Stage 1: Counseling Interview

- The immediate supervisor should advise the employee of his concern over the absences, try to establish the reasons for the sickness and determine what needs to be done to improve attendance.
- If any medical condition is identified at this stage, and is likely to have an effect on job suitability, the supervisor should arrange an appointment with a company-approved doctor. This should be confirmed to the employee in writing within five working days.

- If, from the discussion, the problem does not appear to be due to an underlying unfitness for work, the supervisor should advise the employee that, while the recorded ailments may be genuine, a sustained improvement in attendance is expected or the next stage in the procedure will be taken.

- A review of the attendance will automatically be made each month for the next six months.

Stage 2: First Formal Review (Verbal Warning Stage)

- If the employee's absences continue to worsen following analysis and regular monitoring, he should be invited to attend a formal review meeting with the supervisor.

- The absence record should be detailed in a letter inviting the employee for this interview. The employee should be advised that she is entitled to be represented by a union representative or a colleague as appropriate.

- The purpose of this meeting will be to:

  -continue to discuss the underlying reasons for the absences,

  -advise the employee of the service and cost implications of her absence, and

  -warn the employee (except when deciding to seek medical advice) that if there is not a substantial and sustained improvement, her employment may be terminated because of her inability to maintain an acceptable attendance level. This constitutes the verbal warning.

- Where medical attention is warranted, action must be taken immediately. The meeting is therefore only adjourned to allow this part of the process to be completed. Within five working days, the employee must receive medical advice. The meeting is then reconvened with HR and the doctor's opinion is discussed.

- If the doctor confirms fitness for work, the employee should be warned about the consequences of continued absence.

Stage 3: Second Formal Review (Written Warning Stage)

- Where regular monitoring indicates that no improvement in the absence pattern has occurred a second formal meeting will be arranged with HR.
- The letter inviting the employee to the meeting will include the absence record and, again, advice on representation.
- Any new information given at the meeting regarding ill health or a change in the nature of sickness may need to be assessed by a company-approved doctor.
- The employee should be given the opportunity to explain his or her absence record. If appropriate, the supervisor should inform the employee that a formal written warning is being issued and that this warning will remain in the employee's file for a specified period. A copy of the warning should be issued to the employee and to his/her representative.
- The employee should be informed that failure to comply with the company's attendance expectations, and to improve on the present unacceptable record of absence, will result in the termination of the employee's employment.
- Where fitness for work is in doubt, proceed with redeployment options according to the guidance received by the doctor. Consult with the employee's union representative (if applicable) on the redeployment process and options.

Stage 4: Temporary Suspension from Work

- If, following the implementation of the previous stages of the disciplinary process, no improvement in attendance occurs, management may proceed with a temporary suspension without pay. The intention to suspend should be confirmed in writing with details of start and end dates. A copy of the letter of suspension should be sent to the employee's representative (if applicable).

Stage 5: Termination of Employment

- This is the final stage in the disciplinary process whereby the employee is dismissed for inability to comply with the company's requirements for attendance at work. Dismissal can only take place with the written authorization of a senior manager and HR.

- The letter calling the employee in will, again, include advice on representation and will outline the absence record. The employee should be advised that, as a result of the interview, he or she may be dismissed for incapability to perform work duties.

- Again, the company doctor may have to be consulted if any new information is forthcoming in regard to the employee's health or capacity for work.

- Where redeployment is not possible, or appropriate, consider proceeding with dismissal for reasons of capability. Eligibility for disability benefit will depend on the circumstances of each case.

- If a decision is made to dismiss on the basis of capability, a copy of the letter of dismissal should be sent to the employee's representative (if appropriate).

- The employee may have the right to appeal against dismissal. The appeal should be in line with the company's disciplinary procedures.

Managing Absenteeism

Effectively managing absenteeism, the growing problem of unscheduled absences, requires that the company recognize that the issue is a problem and then develop a plan to address the issue and solve the problem. Recognizing that a problem exists is pretty easy. The number of days of unscheduled absences in a period of time, a year for example, can be counted. If that number is higher than similar companies, is higher than the company goal, or is growing then the company can recognize that they have an unscheduled absenteeism problem.

The less obvious, and harder to measure, aspect is the problems caused the company by the unscheduled absenteeism issue. There will be resentment among the workers who have to "cover" for the absent workers. There will be a decrease in productivity because of the temporary decrease in workforce.

There may be a decrease in quality as less trained workers have to perform specific tasks. These costs grow quickly and it is in the best interest of the business to get them under control quickly with an effective absenteeism management plan.

TIPS TO CURB ABSENTEEISM

1. Monitor employee attendance by maintaining a system (manual or electronic) where all employees have to sign in and sign out of work.
2. Design a comprehensive leave policy that is in line with the company's values and objectives.
3. Encourage punctuality and attendance, and establish a reward system, if possible.
4. Conduct regular health examinations to curb absenteeism due to illness.

Introducing counseling sessions may prove beneficial in curbing absenteeism due to stress.

5. Keep your staff motivated by creating a favorable work environment.
6. Absenteeism maybe difficult to deal with, in a forthright manner. But the management can come up with several rules and policies to keep it under check.

GOVERNANCE MEASURES TO REDUCE ABSENTEEISM

Following the structure of Lewis and Peterson's four elements of governance, the authors recommend a diverse range of interventions and mechanisms to engage stakeholders to more effectively reduce health worker absenteeism. Some of the interventions proposed may not succeed if implemented in isolation; combining multiple efforts will be more likely to produce a positive outcome. In large part, the effectiveness of interventions for improving standards, incentives, and information will ultimately provide the foundation for stakeholders to justify the accountability measures they seek to make.

Standards Encouraging participation to set and communicate standards. Leaders and managers should take a participatory approach to set appropriate human resources (HR) standards related to attendance and other relevant performance management areas that will make workers' and managers' roles more explicit. Professional councils can play a specific role in reviewing and determining reasonable expectations for each cadre and then advocating for these standards. At the facility level, teams should work together to ensure more equitable shifts, so that workers are not unfairly scheduled or resentful of their hours. Once established, a facility's patient/provider bill of rights and hours of operation should be posted, communicating them to lower-literacy populations with visual illustrations and through traditional community channels (e.g., at community meetings, with traditional village chiefs) when possible. These lower-cost efforts will help inform communities about what they should expect and demand of the health workforce in their locale, which will encourage workers to be present.

Improving working conditions. Work climate plays a critical role in health worker motivation and job satisfaction. There are many low-cost interventions that can be implemented at the local level to improve working conditions. In Kenya, facility-based teams assessed their own working conditions and implemented action plans to improve their environment and job satisfaction. These included making waste disposal safer, improving inventory management, creating staff lounges with free tea, painting and refurbishing facilities, posting facility signage, cleaning yards, and offering continuing education opportunities, all of which motivated health workers to come to work and perform well (Capacity Project 2009). Community involvement and contributions to improve the facility can increase health worker motivation and reduce the likelihood of health worker absenteeism, which in turn enhances the quality of the services they access. For example, community health associations in Mali have helped construct clinic staff housing; provide potable water, cleaning, or laundry services for a more hygienic environment; and offer transport for commuting health workers (Hilhorst et al. 2005).

Incentives Implementing effective incentive packages can greatly contribute to health worker motivation and productivity, including reducing absenteeism. This requires a solid comprehension of workers' preferences within specific contexts. Capacity Plus's **Rapid Retention Survey Toolkit** applies an evidence-based method to determine the optimal package of incentives based on health workers' motivational preferences. Providing housing near the workplace has been a helpful incentive in rural settings. In Bangladesh, lower rates of absenteeism were recorded among health workers residing close to the facility compared to health workers living farther away (Chaudhury and Hammer 2003). Evaluating working conditions and worker satisfaction may also reveal reasons for skipping work.

Recognizing dual employment or authorizing certain hours for health workers to conduct private practice can accommodate for the limitations of public-sector remuneration.

Implementing performance-based financing (PBF) can incentivize individuals, teams, or entire facilities. Because these schemes pay based on the results of performance, health workers need to be present and work effectively to receive the financial incentives directly, as a share of a team disbursement or to raise the chances for a facility to receive its eligible benefits. As such, PBF encourages peer-to-peer accountability and increases remuneration and health worker motivation.

Information Customizing HR information systems (HRIS) can assist HR managers with information on absenteeism. Capacity Plus's **HRIS Suite** of free open source software has been used in many countries to facilitate evidence-based decision-making in health workforce planning and management. Version 4.1 of HRIS offers capabilities for district and facility managers to track leave balances and timesheets, and distinguish unexcused absences from approved leave. An integrated electronic payroll helps managers pay workers on time, which can maintain motivation and reduce absenteeism resulting from repeated efforts to obtain paychecks. In eastern Africa, mobile banking has expanded to the rural health worker payroll.

Paying nurses and community workers with mobile money has shown to improve health worker retention and reduce tardiness (Doerr 2012).

Accountability Leveraging political will. Taking a stand to increase health worker productivity through a reduction of absenteeism often requires a high level of commitment and authority as the decision and repercussions can be political in nature. In light of this, stakeholders should evaluate which leaders could be willing to take a stand against absenteeism. To the extent possible, the information they present to these leaders should include the specific factors leading to and consequences of absenteeism in their context, especially in regards to their economic impact and effect on health outcomes. Potential risks and risk mitigation measures should be thoughtfully considered. Advocates for improved accountability measures should consider how the timing of elections and political appointment cycles may affect a leader's willingness to support their cause. Advocacy efforts should also focus on professional councils and associations to engage them in fomenting high levels of professionalism among their cadres and supporting political decisions and appropriate mechanisms to address absenteeism of the health workforce.

Enforcing sanctions Managers and communities should be committed to hold health service providers accountable for their processes and outcomes. Transparency is essential in defining the indicators and processes for enforcing HR standards and applying appropriate disciplinary measures. If standards and rules are established but not enforced, health workers could actually be disincentivized to follow them, which can slowly unravel other efforts to reduce absenteeism. While it is never a pleasant undertaking, sanctions must be imposed if specified outputs and outcomes are not delivered (Lewis and Peterson 2009). Professional councils, managers, and health facility teams can work together to decide what consequences are reasonable for occasional, chronic, and severely chronic absenteeism. Punitive measures should allow for adequate recourse, with step-wise warnings to avoid firing workers and leaving posts vacant for long periods (Vujicic 2010). It may be easier to take small disciplinary measures that respond to minor infractions to set the tone of "zero tolerance" than to impose serious sanctions after absenteeism has been taking place for a long time.

CONTROL OF ABSENTEEISM

Your HR policy on attendance and absenteeism together with your disciplinary rules must make it very clear what will happen in the case of absence without permission or reasonable excuse that is verifiable.

1. Find out whether the absenteeism of an employee is above the "acceptable" average
2. Identify the pattern of absenteeism problems
3. Thoroughly investigate and document
4. Find out whether the problem is due to a medical condition requiring long-term medical attention
5. Verify whether it is likely that the employee will improve his / her attendance record in future
6. Check whether your policies are clear and the employee had been informed
7. Ensure that you had given counseling to the employee and had given him or her an adequate opportunity to improve attendance

Keep in mind that some employees will provide excuse for their non-attendance or absence on their health problems. These employees will misuse medical leave if given the opportunity. Medical leave is usually the most misused benefit.

Steps you can take
1. Establish clear attendance and absenteeism policies
2. Ensure a reliable attendance monitoring system is in place and used effectively by supervisors
3. Implement positive and negative controls
   For example, give value to good attendance and penalize inexcusable absence.

FACTORS INFLUENCING ABSENTEEISM IN A WORKPLACE

Workplace absences always have a personal component to them. This can make it hard for a company to discern the particular cause without having an employee divulge information about his personal life. In specific cases, that may eventually become necessary, but in general companies can fight absenteeism by making it more appealing for their employees to come to work and by showing understanding and lenience when absences occur. In particular, companies should strive to provide their workers with enough pay, enough dignity and a positive enough workplace so that merely showing up each day doesn't wear a worker down.

1. Negative Work Environment

Companies often try to save money by squeezing their employees of pay, benefits, perks and respect. Employees feel this pinch and respond accordingly. For example, if your company overwhelms employees with heavy workloads or doesn't offer enough vacation days, some people will make up for it by taking more sick days. A negative work environment can also take hold when employee relations go sour. Anyone who finds herself chronically frustrated by her coworkers will need to take more days off to manage stress and recuperate.

2. Waning Job Commitment

Even when companies treat their employees decently and maintain a positive work environment, sometimes an employee will still lose interest in his job there. Maybe he has career ambitions elsewhere. Maybe he doesn't like the culture at the company. Whatever the reason, an employee with a waning commitment may begin to show less professionalism at work, including tardiness and absenteeism.

3. Personal Hardships

Every worker faces hardships in her personal life that don't relate to the workplace. From family troubles, to financial woes, to health problems, to substance abuse, problems in an employee's personal life often manifest at work in the form of absenteeism. Companies can and should hold an employee accountable for her performance at work, including attendance, but if they want to retain her they must also strive to show her flexibility and patience. Personal hardships happen, and in many cases they pass soon enough.

4. Full Life

Sometimes employees don't have a hard life so much as a full one. Beginning a family, pursuing an education and maintaining relationships all take up a lot of time. Don't be surprised when an employee sometimes needs more time off even though he has a satisfying life both at work and at home. It happens, and these kinds of successful, happy employees have a lot to offer their employers. Companies that insist their employees put work first and everything else second will lose this kind of talent to companies that respect employees who have a lot to live for.

7 TIPS FOR CONTROLLING AND PREVENTING EMPLOYEE ABSENTEEISM

Absenteeism in the workplace is a problem all managers encounter, and although absences are often due to legitimate reasons, they can get out of control if they're not managed carefully.

Persistent unexcused absenteeism, particularly when it involves just a few individuals, not only lowers productivity and increases everyone else's workload, but it can precipitate a sour atmosphere in the workplace. It's something that needs to be nipped in the bud.

Statistics vary on the monetary impact of absenteeism, but the U.S. Bureau of Labor Statistics says it tends to be highest among service occupations, such as healthcare, food service, cleaning, and so forth, and administrative staff.

Absences occur for many reasons – burnout, stress, low morale, job hunting, etc. – and need to be addressed quickly. The following tips may help:

1. Is the Absence for Genuine Reasons?

Ever wondered if there was a good reason behind that call you just got from an absent employee excusing himself from work for the day? Often there is a genuine reason and your gut instinct can guide you on this one. However, if you are noticing an excessive pattern and finding it hard to take your employee's word for it, then it's time to take action. If an employee is simply not bothering to show up or give you advance notice, then an intervention is essential. Start keeping a paper trail and records of absences.

2. Give Absent Employees an Opportunity to Explain Themselves

The first thing you can do is give employees an opportunity to explain themselves. When they return to work, have a one-on-one discussion about their absence and express your concern. This is not a disciplinary discussion, but more of a fact-finding mission. Your goal is to understand what's happening and try to solve the issue. For example, if stress is a factor, then you may need to discuss strategies that can help, such as shifting workloads, reducing responsibilities, etc.

Very often, employees are pleased that they have been given an opportunity to air their problems or grievances. But be warned, you may learn things that you don't want to hear, particularly if it turns out that your management style is the problem. Try to remain objective during the discussion and use it as a platform to change things.

3. Put a Performance Improvement Plan in Place

If the tactic above doesn't work, then you need to put a performance review plan in place that sets specific goals for improvement, attendance being one of them. Put the plan in writing and clearly explain the timeframe of the plan and the consequences of not fulfilling its requirements.

4. Develop and Communicate a Clear Leave / Sick Leave Policy

A written policy won't stop absenteeism, but it will help you deal with it more effectively. It will also demonstrate to all employees that you don't tolerate absenteeism. Use the document to clearly explain paid and unpaid leave policies and the consequences of unexcused absences. If you have a company newsletter or intranet, use these to promote your policy.

Note that the law doesn't require you to provide common leave benefits, but it does require employers to provide leave under the Family and Medical Leave

Act (FMLA). Be sure you know what the law is. Read more about the FMLA leave entitlement qualifying medical events in S A's Employee enefits Guide (scroll down to "Leave Policy").

5. Assess your Management Style

It's hard to acknowledge, but one of the more common reasons for employee dissatisfaction is management style. Could your style be encouraging employees to harbor grudges or lose morale? Step back and assess what you can do differently. Is your open door policy really that open? Do employees really feel valued? Plan on setting side more management time for your team, discuss their professional goals, and share your vision for the continued growth of your business and their role in it. For tips on assessing your management style and ideas to shake it up some, read 4 Tips for Effective and Inspiring Business Leadership.

6. Consider Introducing Incentive Plans

While their are no guarantees that you can control absenteeism, initiatives such as incentive plans and programs such as flex-time, wellness programs, and project completion perks, are proven to increase morale and productivity. They also send a clear message to your employees that they have a recognized and valuable role to play in your business as a whole. The following articles have tips on how to recognize, nurture, and incentivize employees:

- Get More from Your Team - 5 Employee Incentive Program Ideas That Pay Off
- Recognizing Performance in a Tough Economy: How to Best Reward Stand-Out Employees

7. Terminating Repeat Offenders

If you've exhausted all these intervention measures and aren't seeing improvement, then termination may be your only option. Follow your HR policy to the letter on this one and refer to the law as it pertains to terminating employees, final pay checks, and more.

EMPLOYEE ABSENTEEISM - WHAT CAN ONE DO ABOUT IT?

Excessive absenteeism can be costly for business in terms of both replacement costs and lost productivity. If not managed properly, chronic offenders can also be a source of frustration for those employees who generally do the right thing.

BELOW ARE SIX THINGS THAT YOU CAN DO TO IMPROVE ATTENDANCE IN THE WORKPLACE:

1. Make Employees Aware of Expectations

Make sure employees are aware of attendance expectations and the effects of excessive absenteeism on the business including remaining team members, productivity and customer service. This sort of information should be made clear at an employee's induction and reinforced through your employee manual, code of conduct and/or Personal/Career's Leave policy.

2. Analyze Attendance Records

Analyze attendance records to properly identify the extent of employee absence and any particular trends. For example, employees who seem to always be off on a Monday or a Friday or before or after a public holiday. There is no law against confronting an employee and asking for an explanation as to why their absences mostly seem to occur on particular days.

3. Have a Clear Policy in Place

Have a clear policy and procedure that employees must follow if they are going to be absent. For example, you could state that employees:

a. Make direct contact with a manager or someone in authority to advise of their absence, the nature of their illness and when they expect to return. Do not allow employees to just speak with the receptionist or send email or text messages to a work colleague. If an employee is not genuine about being sick, they may think twice if they are required to speak directly with the boss.

b. Are expected to make contact by a certain time or within a specified time period.

c. Are required to provide evidence of their illness which may be a Doctor's Certificate or Statutory Declaration. Note: The Fair Work Act 2009 no longer requires an employee to produce a medical certificate or statutory declaration. Instead, the Personal/Career's Leave National Employment Standard ("NES") requires that employees provide evidence that would satisfy a "reasonable person" of their unfitness for work. Therefore, it may not be considered reasonable to expect employees to produce a medical certificate for every single day absent unless the sick leave is excessive or there is a clear pattern of single day absences e.g. Fridays and Mondays or every second Thursday etc. Given the NES does not define "reasonable" it is timely to ensure that your business has a clear policy in place which defines what evidence requirements are expected of employees. Additionally, the NES provides that an Enterprise Agreement or Modern Award may specify evidence requirements in relation to Personal/Career's leave.

4. Make Employees Aware of the Consequences

Make employees aware of the consequences of not adhering to your Personal/Career's leave policy which may include disciplinary action. Remember to focus on whether the employee has followed the correct notice and evidence procedures rather than try and establish whether the person was genuinely sick or not. Only a Doctor is qualified to do that!

5. Follow Up With Employees Upon Their Return

Follow up with employees face to face when they return to work and enquire about their wellness and whether they are fit to resume normal duties. This lets the employee know that you are concerned about their well-being and that you have "noticed" their absence.

6. Identify Any Hidden Causes

Identify any hidden causes. Often poor attendance is just a symptom of a greater problem and not the real cause. Aside from common illness, there can be many reasons why an employee is taking excessive sick leave:

- Drug and alcohol problems
- Issues with a work colleague or supervisor
- Not coping with workload or some other aspect of their work
- Family/marital issues
- Work/Life Balance

Before launching into disciplinary action, it makes good sense to speak with the employee concerned and try to uncover the root cause of the problem. You may then be able to determine some strategies to address the situation.

MANGO PROCESSING INDUSTRY OF INDIA

INTRODUCTION

Mango is a fruit which has many varieties and is grown in majority of the states of the country. Pulp or juice of ripe mangoes is consumed along with main course. Many taste enriches are made from unripe mangoes and their shelf life is enhanced either by processing them or by using preservatives. Pickles, chutneys and many sweet preparations like murabba are made from unripe or semi-ripe mangoes. This fruit is available only during 4-5 months every year and is generally liked by everyone. Mangoes are grown all over the country and Bihar and Jharkhand states have ample production of mangoes and thus mango processing can be started after assessing the market.

PRODUCT

Mango processing is a traditional activity and products like pickle, chutney, murabba are consumed throughout the year. Every region has its own taste or liking and a care has to be taken to understand it and accordingly the recipe has to be finalized. Compliance with FPO and PFA Act is necessary.

MARKET POTENTIAL

Indians are fond of table enriches, which are regularly used along with the main course as well as snacks. Apart from individual households, restaurants, eateries, roadside dhabas, clubs, hostels, caterers etc. are the bulk consumers. There are some branded products available in the market but they are costly. The real competition would be from the age-old practice of making pickles or chutneys or murabba domestically. Many Indian households make these items during the season. But this practice is gradually disappearing due to changing lifestyles, hassles of making these items and their availability throughout the year from market. There are many

- 51 -

variants of these products and with certain change in the ingredients, taste differs. Hence, it is imperative to cater to the regional palate.

MANUFACTURING PROCESS

It is very well standardized. In case of pickles, unripe mangoes are washed and cut into small pieces and then salt and turmeric powder is applied on it and then these pieces are sun-dried for couple of hours. Then mango pieces and other ingredients like methi powder, spices etc. are thoroughly mixed with edible oil and finally packing is undertaken. Mango chutney is prepared after washing mangoes and cutting them into small pieces. Then they are cooked

With spices and after adding sugar and vinegar, it is packed. Murabba is prepared from pieces of mango. These pieces are soaked in lemon water for couple of hours and then O washed. Then they are cooked with sugar syrup at around 60-65 C and packed. along with sugar syrup after cooling. Removal of seed and process waste account for 35% loss.

ORIGIN

Cultivation of mango is believed to have originated in S.E. Asia. Mango is being cultivated in southern Asia for nearly six thousand years.

AREA & PRODUCTION

India ranks first among world's mango producing countries accounting for about 50 of the world's mango production. Other major mango producing countries include China, Thailand, Mexico, Pakistan, Philippines, Indonesia, Brazil, Nigeria and Egypt. India's share is around 52 of world production i.e. 12 million tonnes as against world's production of 23 million tonnes (2002-03).

An increasing trend has been observed in world mango production averaging 22 million metric tonnes per year. Worldwide production is mostly concentrated in Asia, accounting for 75% followed by South and Northern America with about 10% share.

Area under cultivation and production trends of mangoes in India during 1997-98 to 2001-02 are depicted in graphs 1 & 2. Major producing States are Andhra Pradesh, Bihar, Gujarat, Karnataka, Maharashtra, Orissa, Tamil Nadu, Uttar Pradesh and West Bengal. Other States where mangoes are grown include Madhya Pradesh, Kerala, Haryana, Punjab etc.

The crop accounts for 39% of area under fruit corps in India and 23% of production of these crops.

ECONOMIC IMPORTANCE

The fruit is very popular with the masses due to its wide range of adaptability, high nutritive value, richness in variety, delicious taste and excellent flavour. It is a rich source of vitamin A and C. The fruit is consumed raw or ripe. Good mango varieties contain 20% of total soluble sugars. The acid content of ripe desert fruit varies from 0.2 to 0.5 % and protein content is about 1 %.

Raw fruits of local varieties of mango trees are used for preparing various traditional products like raw slices in brine, amchur, pickle, murabba, chutney, panhe (sharabat) etc. Presently, the raw fruit of local varieties of mango are used for preparing pickle and raw slices in brine on commercial scale while fruits of Alphonso variety are used for squash in coastal western zone.

The wood is used as timber, and dried twigs are used for religious purposes. The mango kernel also contains about 8-10% good quality fat which can be used for saponification. Its starch is used in confectionery industry.

Mango also has medicinal uses. The ripe fruit has fattening, diuretic and laxative properties. It helps to increase digestive capacity.

MARKET ANALYSIS AND STRATEGY
Demand and Supply patterns; World Trade

Among internationally traded tropical fruits, mango ranks only second to pineapple in quantity and value. Major markets for fresh and dried mangoes in 1998 were: Malaysia, Japan, Singapore, Hong Kong and the Netherlands, while for canned mango were: Netherlands, Australia, United Kingdom, Germany, France and USA.

Southeast Asian buyers consume mangoes all year round. Their supplies come mainly from India, Pakistan, Indonesia, Thailand, Malaysia, Philippines, Australia and most recently South Africa.

Each exporting country has its own varieties, which differ in shape, colour and flavour. Prices are very low for Indonesian and Thailand fruit and are on the higher side for Indian fruit. In the United States of America, the prices vary with the season, higher prices found during February and March, when mango availability is lowest.

Most international trade in fresh mangoes takes place within short distances. Mexico, Haiti and razil account for the majority of North America's imports. **India and Pakistan are the predominant suppliers to the West Asian market.** Southeast Asian countries get most of their supplies from the Philippines and Thailand. European Union buyers source mangoes from

South America and Asia. Although Asia accounts for 75 percent of world production, its dominance does not translate into international trade.

INTERNATIONAL MARKETS FOR INDIAN MANGO

Asian producers find it easier to expand sales to the European Union. Europe's acceptance of different varieties is greater, because of a large demand from Asian immigrant groups. Phytosanitary restrictions are less stringent. Transportation costs are not as big a factor in exporting mangoes to the European Union as in exporting to the United States market: for example, India and Pakistan are able to compete with non-Asian suppliers to the European Union, whereas proximity gives Mexico and Haiti a clear advantage in supplying to the United States market.

Fifty-four percent of European Union imports enter during the periods May to July and November to December, with peak imports in June. French imports reach peak in April and May, whereas United Kingdom imports are concentrated during the May to July. German imports are spread more evenly throughout the year. Of the top suppliers, Brazil provided chiefly during the period November to December, the United States during June to October, South Africa during January to April and Venezuela during April to July. Pakistan supplies the majority of its exports to the European Union during June and July;

Indian exports take place mainly during the month of May.

Although a lion's share of Indian mango goes to the Gulf countries, efforts are being made to exploit European, American and Asian markets. About 13,000 MT of Alphonso variety is exported to Middle East, UK and Netherlands every year.

The different products of mango which are exported include mango chutney, pickles, jam, squash, pulp, juice, nectar and slices. These are being exported to U.K., U.S.A., Kuwait and Russia. Besides these, the fresh mangoes are being exported to Bangladesh, Bahrain, France, Kuwait, Malaysia, Nepal, Singapore and U.K.

The varieties in demand at the international market include Kent, Tomy Atkin, Alphonso and Kesar. Varieties such as Alphonso, Dashehari, Kesar, Banganapalli and several other varieties that are currently in demand in the international markets are produced and exported from India.

'Mahamango', a co-operative society was established in 1991 with the support of Maharashtra State Agricultural & Marketing Board (Pune). This was mainly formed to boost the export of Alphonso mangoes as well as for domestic marketing. Facilities like pre-cooling, cold storages, pack house, grading packing line etc. have been made available at the facility centre of Mahamango for which the financial assistance was given by APEDA, New Delhi and Maharashtra State Agricultural & Marketing Board (Pune).

A similar type of association named 'MANGROW' has been formed for the export of Kesar mangoes from Aurangabad district of Maharashtra.

IMPORT/EXPORT TRENDS

India's mango exports were estimated at 45 thousand tonnes worth Rs 100 crore (Rs 1 billion) in 2002-03. Fresh mangoes are exported to Bangladesh, U.A.E., Saudi Arabia and U.K. and mango pulp to U.A.E., Saudi Arabia, Kuwait, Netherlands, U.S.A and U.K. Processed mango products viz. pickle and chutney are exported to U.K., U.A.E., Saudi Arabia, Germany, Netherlands, U.S.A and U.K.

TABLE NO. 3.1

Country-wise export of mangoes from India during 2001-02

Country	Quantity ('000 Tonnes)	Value (Rs. in crores)
Bangladesh	21.03	24.10
U.A.E	12.81	28.19
Saudi Arabia	02.94	06.62
U.K.	01.37	04.54
Kuwait0	00.98	03.10
Oman	00.88	01.88
U.S.A.	00.73	01.63
Bahrain	00.60	02.01
Others	03.09	08.92
Total	**44.43**	**80.99**

Source: APEDA, New Delhi

The biggest importer of mango is the United States importing an average of 1, 85,000 metric tonnes annually (about 45% of the total world import volume). Europe's top importers of mango include Netherlands, France, UK, Germany and Belgium with an aggregate average volume of 95,000 metric tonnes imported annually.

Of late Asian market has been expanding. China's market has been increasing and ranks second among the top importers in the world. Other Asian markets such as Malaysia, UAE, Saudi Arabia and Singapore have been among the top ten importers exhibiting an export growth average of 20% annually.

Analysis and Future Strategy

Mango has an established export market and poses bright opportunities for export in the international market whether in fresh or processed forms. Similarly, the mango industry has provided livelihood opportunities to its growers and those involved in its marketing channel. **Creation of essential infra-structure** for preservation, cold storage, refrigerated transportation, rapid transit, grading, processing, packaging and quality control are the important aspects which needs more attention.

There is need for developing processing industries in the southern region of the country where post harvest losses in handling and marketing are higher.

There is scope to establish mango preservation factories in cooperative sector. Mango growers' cooperatives on the lines of Mahamango need to be encouraged to come up in major mango producing States. This will add to their income through processing and create additional employment opportunities for the rural people.

Considerable amount of waste material, e.g., mango stones, peels remain unutilized which can be used properly by the processors to earn more profit.

PRODUCTION TECHNOLOGY

Agro-climatic requirements

Mango is well adapted to tropical and sub-tropical climates. It thrives well in almost all the regions of the country but cannot be grown commercially in areas above 600 m. It cannot stand severe frost, especially when the tree is young. High temperature by itself is not so injurious to mango, but in combination with low humidity and high winds, it affects the tree adversely.

Mango varieties usually thrive well in places with rainfall in the range of 75-375 cm. /annum and dry season. The distribution of rainfall is more important than its amount. Dry weather before blossoming is conducive to profuse flowering. Rain during flowering is detrimental to the crop as it interferes with pollination. However, rain during fruit development is good but heavy rains cause damage to ripening fruits. Strong winds and cyclones during fruiting season can play havoc as they cause excessive fruit drop.

Loamy, alluvial, well drained, aerated and deep soils rich in organic matter with a pH range of 5.5 to 7.5 are ideal for mango cultivation.

Growing and Potential Belts

Mango is cultivated in almost all the states of India. The state-wise growing belts are given in the following:

TABLE NO. 3.2

State-Wise Growing Belts

State	Growing belts
Andhra Pradesh	Krishna, East and West Godavari, Vishakhapatnam, Srikakulam, Chittoor, Adilabad, Khamman, Vijaynagar
Chhattisgarh	Jabalpur, Raipur, Bastar
Gujarat	Bhavnagar, Surat, Valsad, Junagarh, Mehsana, Khera
Haryana	Karnal, Kurushetra
Jammu & Kashmir	Jammu, Kathwa, Udhampur
Jharkhand	Ranchi, Sindega, Gumla, Hazaribagh, Dumka, Sahibganj, Godda.

Karnataka	Kolar, Bangalore, Tumkur, Kagu
Kerala	Kannur, Palakkad, Trissur, Malappuram
Madhya Pradesh	Rewa, Satna, Durg, Bilaspur, Bastar, Ramnandgaon, Rajgari, Jabalpur, Katni, Balagha
Maharashtra	Ratnagiri, Sindhudurg, Raigarh
Orissa	Sonepur, Bolangir, Gajapati, Koraput, Rayagada, Gunpur, Malkanpuri, Dhenkanal, Ganjam, Puri
Punjab	Gurdaspur, Hoshiarpur, Ropar
Tamil Nadu	Dharmapuri, Vellore, Tiruvallur, Theni, Madurai
Uttaranchal	Almora, Nainital, Dehradun, Bageshwar, UdhamSingh Nagar, Haridwar
Uttar Pradesh	Saharanpur, Bulandshahar, Lucknow, Faizabad, Varanasi
West Bengal	Malda, Murshidabad, Nadia

Varieties Cultivated

In India, about 1,500 varieties of mango are grown including 1,000 commercial varieties. Each of the main varieties of mango has an unique taste and flavour.

Based on time of ripening , varieties may be classified as under :

Early	-	Bombai, Bombay Green , Himsagar, Kesar, Suvernarekha
Mid-season	-	Alphonso, Mankurad, Bangalora, Vanraj, Banganapalli, Dashehari, Langra, Kishen Bhog, Zardalu, Mankurad
Late	-	Fazli, Fernandin, Mulgoa, Neelum, Chausa

Hybrids:

Amrapalli (Dashehari x Neelum), Mallika (Neelum x Dashehari), Arka Aruna (Banganapalli x Alphonso), Arka Puneet (Alphonso x Janardhan Pasand), Arka Neelkiran (Alpohonso x Neelum), Ratna (Neelum x Alphonso), Sindhu (Ratna x Alphonso), Au Rumani (Rumani x Mulgoa), Manjeera (Rumani x Neelum), PKM 1 (Chinnasuvernarekha x Neelum), Alfazli, Sunder Langra, Sabri, Jawahar, Neelphonso, Neeleshan, Neeleshwari, PKM 2 (very few of these hybrid varieties are grown commercially in the country).

The important mango varieties cultivated in different states of India are given below :

State	Varieties grown
Andhra Pradesh	- Allumpur Baneshan, Banganapalli, Bangalora, Cherukurasam, Himayuddin, Suvernarekha, Neelum, Totapuri
Bihar	- Bathua, Bombai, Himsagar, Kishen Bhog, Sukul, Gulab Khas, Zardalu, Langra, Chausa, Dashehari, Fazli
Goa	- Fernandin, Mankurad
Gujarat	- Alphonso, Kesar, Rajapuri, Vanraj, Jamadar, Totapuri, Neelum, Dashehari, Langra
Haryana	- Dashehari, Langra, Sarauli, Chausa, Fazli
Himachal Pradesh	- Chausa, Dashehari, Langra
Jharkhand	- Jardalu, Amrapalli, Mallika, Bombai, Langra, Himsagar, Chausa, Gulabkhas
Karnataka	- Alphonso, Bangalora, Mulgoa, Neelum, Pairi, Baganapalli, Totapuri
Kerala	- Mundappa, Olour, Pairi

Madhya Pradesh	-	Alphonso, Bombay Green, Langra, Sunderja, Dashehari, Fazli, Neelum, Amrapalli, Mallika
Maharashtra	-	Alphonso, Mankurad, Mulgoa, Pairi, Rajapuri, Kesar, Gulabi, Vanraj
Orissa	-	Baneshan, Langra, Neelum, Suvarnarekha, Amrapalli, Mallika
Punjab	-	Dashehari, Langra, Chausa, Malda
Rajasthan	-	Bombay Green, Chausa, Dashehari, Langra
Tamil Nadu	-	Banganapalli, Bangalora, Neelum, Rumani, Mulgoa, Alphonso, Totapuri
Uttar Pradesh	-	Bombay Green, Dashehari, Langra, Safeda Lucknow, Chausa, Fazli
West Bengal	-	Bombai, Himsagar, Kishen Bhog, Langra, Fazli, Gulabkhas, Amrapalli, Mallika

MANGO PULP

These are made from selected varieties of Mango. Fully matured Mangoes are harvested, quickly transported to our fruit processing plant, inspected and washed. Selected high quality fruits go to the controlled ripening chambers Fully Ripened Mango fruits are then washed, blanched, pulped, reseeded, centrifuged, homogenized, concentrated when required, thermally processed and aseptically filled maintaining commercial sterility.

ALPHONSO MANGO PULP

We are one of the foremost mango pulp manufacturers in India. We manufacture mango pulps like **Alphonso Mango Pulp**. Our natural alphonso mango pulp are known for their wondrous quality level. Alphonso

Mango Pulp is extracted by commercial processing of properly Matured, Sound, Cleaned and Ripened Alphonso Mango Fruits.

Technical Specifications

- Total Soluble Solids (Brix) Minimum 16° Degree
- Acidity as C.A % 0.5 - 0.85%
- pH 3.5 - 3.8
- Pulp Content 96 - 100%
- Color and Appearance Golden Yellow
- Viscosity (Ford Cup No. 8) 40-45 Sec
- Vacuum Minimum7" Hg
- Taste and Flavour Characteristic Flavour of natural Ripe Alphonso
- Mango Fruit
- Net Weight 3.1 Kg
- Gross Weight 3.4 Kg
- Impurities Practically free from black specs and fiber. Not more than 5 specs per 10g of pulp.

OTAPURI MANGO PULP

Have you experienced mesmerizing taste of **Totapuri Mango Pulp**. If not, then just come to us as we are one of the major sweetened totapuri mango pulp suppliers in India. Our natural totapuri mango pulp are really great in taste!

Totapuri Mango Pulp is extracted by commercial processing of properly Matured, Sound, Cleaned and Ripened Totapuri Mango Fruits.

Technical Specifications

- Total Soluble Solids (Brix) Minimum 14° Degree
- Acidity as C.A % 0.045 - 0.05%
- pH 3.5 - 4
- Pulp Content 96 - 100%
- Color and Appearance Turmeric Yellow
- Viscosity (Ford Cup No. 8) 35-45 Sec
- Vacuum Minimum 7" Hg
- Taste and Flavour Characteristic Flavour of natural Ripe Totapuri Mango Fruit
- Net Weight 3.1 Kg
- Gross Weight 3.4 Kg
- Impurities Practically free from black specs and fiber.
- Not more than 5 specs per 10g of pulp

FROZEN MANGO PULP

We offer **Frozen Mango Pulp** that is prepared from fresh mangoes. The Frozen Mango Pulp that we manufacture, export and Supply is fresh and juicy. The Frozen Mango Pulp offered by us is available throughout the year and can be used for consumption at any time. Moreover, we provide Mango Pulp in proper packaging and at reasonable price.

COMPANY PROFILE

RMM food products were established more than 50 years ago. We are the leading growers, wholesalers, exporters of fruits, fruit pulp, fruit juices and other allied products in India. The experience and strength we have in the fruit industry gives us the advantage over others in terms of quality. The best tasting drink in a very appealing packaging makes spires (our drink brand) a winner.

Tasa Foods has been recognized as the forerunner in being the leading manufacturers and exporters of fruit purees and concentrates in South India. Ever since produced the finest and purest fruit purees and concentrate in India. The Tasa Foods has been recognized as the forerunner in being the leading manufacturers and exporters of fruit purees and concentrates in South India. Tasa Group started its operations with the initiative taken by Late Mr. R.M Muneer, in the year 1968. It has risen to be the largest fruit supply company in India, supplying fruits to the entire fruit processing industry for the last four decades even to the international markets. The global clientele includes Africa, Asia, America and Europe.

At Tasa Foods, a conventional ripening process is implemented to produce the world's best tasting fruits with the right blend of temperature and atmospheric conditions. We firmly believe in delivering top notch products and utilize the latest agricultural technologies and state of the art farming & production methods with the world class machineries.

We utilize the state of the art technology and maintain international standards and specifications to meet our client's exacting demands. Over the years we have been able to integrate, test & develop methods to achieve the finest and the tastiest fruit pulp and puree products. Tasa Food's unmatched track record, passion for quality & consistency has seen its unmatched elevation.

Our infrastructure, policies, quality processes, source location traceability, effective logistics and our efficient team help us cater to the ever growing demand for more fruit pulp every season.

Unique facilities are still implemented where traditional methods handed down a generous dose of wisdom that meets modern technology to ensure the best ripening procedures. Temperature, light, atmosphere and other factors are all carefully blended to produce the finest quality fruit pulp. At Tasa Foods, we believe in following natural processes as much as possible, as its not only eco friendly, but fruits taste their best when this process is followed.

Tasa Foods ensures that the products are delivered to all customers fresh like our brand says it "TASA" which means fresh.

Mangoes have been cultivated in India for thousands of years. The mango is native to the Indian subcontinent from where it was distributed worldwide.

The mango is generally sweet, although the taste and texture of the flesh varies across cultivars. Mango fruit is an excellent source of Vitamin-A and flavonoids like beta-carotene, alpha-carotene, and beta-cryptoxanthin.

Quality

We lay immense emphasis on the quality of food products manufactured at our unit. Quality in the food products can be achieved only if strict quality norms are followed in the whole processing, right from the procurement of raw materials to the final packaging of the product.

Infrastructure

We have a large unit for production which is spread about more than 55,000 square feet of area. For qualitative production, we have installed latest machineries at our manufacturing unit. We have a team of efficient employees including supervisors and quality checkers.

Staff Facility

We strongly believe in investing into Leadership & Development of our employees. Towards this end, we provide our personnel with

> Uniforms

> In depth Technical Training

> Health Programs

> Safety Programs

> Hygienic Cafeteria & Pantry

> Recreation Area

> Further Education Programs

> Counseling

Main Markets

> North America

> South America

> Western Europe

> Eastern Europe

> Eastern Asia

> Southeast Asia

> Mid East

> Africa

> Oceania

Tasa Foods houses a complete training facility for all its staffers. We ensure every personnel in the organization undergo the training program and are certified internally to meet the international standards. We train our staff regularly with a strong backend knowledge base to help them upgrade with new machinery and processes timely. Our employee induction programs are a feature to reckon with, where the employee learns & participates in vital Team Building activities, Corporate Social Responsibility and various other important modules. We have created a unique blend of professionals-a great team, with the best experience in the industry and new comers who have the potential for new innovative thinking. We motivate our team with rewards & recognition activities, and hold health and yoga camps for our employees to maintain work life balance.

Products & Services

Ready to serve fruit drinks (mango, guava, grape, pineapple)

Certification

SGF-IRMA CERTIFIED

Safeguarding the quality of the raw materials International Raw Material Assurance IRMA

ISO 22000 CERTIFIED , Food Safety Management System, ISO 220002005 Incorporation HACCP Principles

HALAL CERTIFIED

KOSHER CERTIFIED, Food Safety Management System

FSSAI CERTIFIED

Facilities

Tasa Foods has two state of the art processing plants located in Chittoor. We have in house laboratory providing chemical, microbiological and analytical services

SPECIFICATIONS OF FRUIT PUREES & CONCENTRATES

Product   Alphonso Mango Puree (16-20 Brix)

Variety   Gujarat/ Maharashtra/ Karnataka
Origin   India

Parameter Group	Range Value
PHYSICAL & CHEMICAL	
Refract metric Bricks @ 20 Deg Cell	16 - 20 Bricks
Acidity As % Any. Citric Acid	0.50-0.90%
pH As Natural	<4.0
Consistency – Bootlick	9-15 cams/30 sacs
Bricks – Acid Ratio	18 – 32
Specific Gravity	1.061
Black Specks / 10 gm	NIL
Brown Specks / 10 gm	<10
MICROBIOLOGICAL	
Total Plate Count cru/ gm	<50
Yeast & Mould Count cru / gm	<20
Coli form Count cru / gm	Absent
Pathogens cru / gm	Absent
ORGANOLEPTIC	
Color	Oranges Yellow

Flavor & Aroma	Characteristics of Typical Ripe Alphorns Mango
Taste	Characteristics of Typical Ripe Alphorns Mango
	Free of Any Fermentation Or Any Other Off Taste.
Appearance	Homogenous, No Foreign Matter

PACKING

220 Liters Aseptic Bag-In-Drums – 215 Kegs Nett

3.10 Kegs A – 10 OTS Cans X 6Nos X1 Carton – 18.600 Kegs Nett

CONTAINER LOADING

Bag – In – Drums – 80 Drums / 20 Ft Fall

Can – In – Cartons – 1000 Cartons / 20 Ft Fall

STORAGE

Recommended Storage Temp = + 10 Deg. Cell.

Maximum Storage Temp = +25 Deg. Cell.

SHELF – LIFE

24 Months @ + 10 Deg. Cell.

FUNCTIONS OF OFFICE OF SPECIAL CONCERNS

1. Coordinate all sectors clients of the office such CSOs, MNLF, MILF, Traditional Leaders, Religious, Women, and Youth including the Indigenous Peoples.

2. Assess and evaluate the issues and concerns of the above sectors being referred to the ORGV and recommend appropriate action

3. May propose programs. Projects and activities for consideration

4. Coordinate with the Concerned Agencies of ARMM for possible programs and Projects for each sector.

5. Assist the above sectors in establishing links with concerned offices including foreign funding agencies

6. Assist in the monitoring of programs and projects in the ARMM areas.

7. Consolidate all the issues and concerns submitted by the field staff

8. Submit periodic report to the OIC-Regional Vice Governor through her Chief of Staff

MNLF/MILF

1. Conduct of Peace Forum (Central Committee, State Committees

2. Assist in the coordination with the law enforcement agencies for the maintenance of peace and order

3. Assist in the preparation and submission of proposal for possible programs, projects, and/or livelihood assistance

4. Assist in the settlement of Fronts dispute

5. Submit periodic report to the OIC-Regional Vice Governor through her Chief of Staff

FIGURE NO 3.1

OFFICE OF THE REGIONAL VICE GOVERNOR
AUTONOMOUS REGION IN MUSLIM MINDANAO

ORGANIZATIONAL STRUCTURE

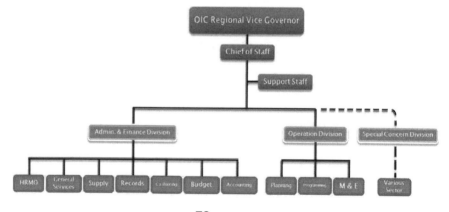

FIGURE NO 3.2
OFFICE ON SPECIAL CONCERNS

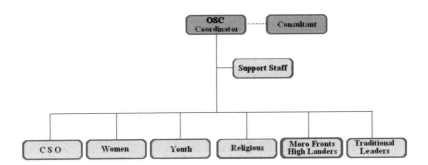

CSO

1. Conduct of CSO Assembly
2. Monitor programs, projects and activities implementation in ARMM areas
3. Assist in the preparation and submission of proposal for possible programs, projects, and/or livelihood assistance
4. Coordinate with the LCEs in the ARMM areas
5. Submit periodic report to the OIC-Regional Vice Governor through her Chief of Staff

Religious

1. Facilitate conduct of Interfaith Dialogue
2. Facilitate conduct of Islamic Value Formation training
3. Assist in the settlements of conflicts

Highlander/Lumad

1. Assist in addressing the concerns of the indigenous people
2. Assist in the settlement of conflicts

Women

1. Assist the women sector in coordinating their social concerns to concerned agencies of the government
2. Assist the women sector in the celebration of the women's month

Youth

1. Assist the youth in coordinating their concerns to appropriate agencies of the ARMM
2. Facilitate acquisition of sports equipments such as balls, rings, etc.
3. Facilitate conduct of Interfaith Dialogue
4. Facilitate conduct of Islamic Value Formation training
5. Assist in the settlements of conflicts

OPINION OF EMPLOYEES WITH REGARD TO ABSENCE BECAUSE OF UNEXPECTED WORK

TABLE - 4.1

OPINION OF EMPLOYEES WITH REGARD TO EMPLOYEES' ABSENCE DUE TO UNEXPECTED WORK

Opinions	No. of Respondents	Percentage
Rarely	97	80
Sometimes	17	15
Always	0	0
Never	6	5
Total	120	100

FIGURE - 4.1

GRAPHICAL REPRESENTATION OF OPINION OF EMPLOYEES' ABSENCE DUE TO UNEXPECTED WORK

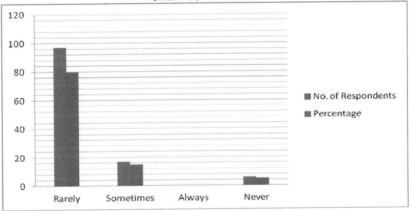

The above table and figure 4.1 depicts that 80% of the employees opined that they are rarely absent because of unexpected work, 15% opined sometimes and 5% opined that they were never absent because of unexpected work.

Hence it can be concluded that most of the employees are rarely absent because of unexpected work.

OPINION OF EMPLOYEES REGARDING HEALTH AS ONE OF THE REASON TO ABSTAIN FROM DUTY

TABLE - 4.2

OPINION OF EMPLOYEES REGARDING GETTING ABSENT TO THE EMPLOYMENT DUE TO HEALTH

Opinions	No. of Respondents	Percentage
Rarely	90	74
Some Times	27	23
Always	0	0
Never	3	3
Total	120	100

FIGURE - 4.2

GRAPHICAL REPRESENTATION OF THE OPINION OF EMPLOYEES REGARDING GETTING ABSENT TO THE EMPLOYMENT DUE TO HEALTH

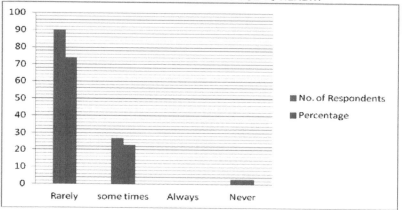

The above table and figure 4.2 depicts that 74% of the employees opined that they are rarely absent because of health reasons, 23% opined sometimes and 3% opined that they were never absent because of health reasons.

Hence it can be concluded that most of the employees are rarely absent because of health.

OPINION OF EMPLOYEES ON TAKING LEAVE WITHOUT PERMISSION

TABLE - 4.3

OPINION OF EMPLOYEES IN TAKING LEAVE WITHOUT PERMISSION

Opinions	No. of Respondents	Percentage
Always	4	4
Never	116	96
Sometimes	0	0
Total	120	100

FIGURE - 4.3

GRAPHICAL REPRESENTATION OF THE OPINION OF EMPLOYEES IN TAKING LEAVE WITHOUT PERMISSION

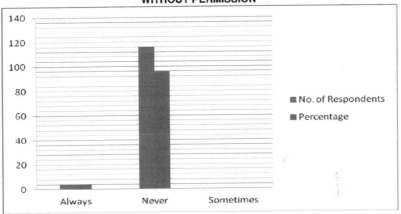

The above table and figure 4.3 depicts that 96% of the employees opined that they never take leave without permission, 4% opined that they always take leave without permission.

Hence it can be concluded that most of the employees never absent themselves without taking permission.

OPINION OF EMPLOYEES ON COMPENSATION FOR THE WORK THEY PERFORM

TABLE - 4.4

OPINION OF EMPLOYEES ON COMPENSATION FOR THE WORK THEY PERFORM

Opinions	No. of Respondents	Percentage
Highly satisfied	17	15
Satisfied	103	85
Neutral	0	0
Dissatisfied	0	0
Highly dissatisfied	0	0
Total	120	100

FIGURE - 4.4

GRAPHICAL REPRESENTATION OF THE OPINION OF EMPLOYEES ON COMPENSATION FOR THE WORK THEY PERFORM

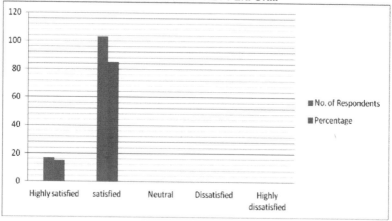

The above table and figure 4.4 depicts that 85% of the employees opined satisfied with the compensation paid for the work they perform and 15% of the employees opined that they are highly satisfied with the compensation paid for the work they perform.

Hence it can be concluded that most of the employees are satisfied with the compensation paid for the work they perform.

EMPLOYEES OPINION ON THE WORKING ENVIRONMENT PROVIDED BY THE ORGANIZATION

TABLE - 4.5

EMPLOYEE OPINION ON THE WORKING ENVIRONMENT IN THE ORGANIZATION

Opinions	No. of Respondents	Percentage
Highly satisfied	40	34
Satisfied	80	66
Neutral	0	0
Dissatisfied	0	0
Highly dissatisfied	0	0
Total	120	100

FIGURE - 4.5

GRAPHICAL REPRESENTATION OF EMPLOYEE OPINION ON THE WORKING ENVIRONMENT IN THE ORGANISATION

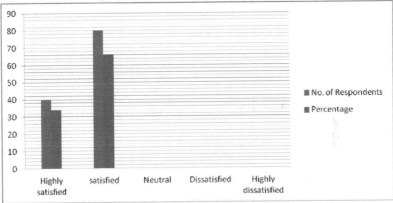

The above table and figure 4.5 depicts that 66% of the employees opined satisfied with the working environment provided by the organization and 34% of the employees opined that they are highly satisfied with the working environment provided by the organization.

Hence it can be concluded that most of the employees are satisfied with the working environment provided by the organization.

OPINION OF THE EMPLOYEES WITH REGARD TO THE RELATIONSHIP WITH SUPERVISOR

TABLE - 4.6

OPINION OF EMPLOYEES ON THEIR RELATIONSHIP WITH SUPERVISOR

Opinions	No. of Respondents	Percentage
Highly satisfied	42	35
Satisfied	78	65
Neutral	0	0
Dissatisfied	0	0
Highly dissatisfied	0	0
Total	120	100

FIGURE - 4.6

GRAPHICAL REPRESENTATION OF THE OPINION OF EMPLOYEES ON THEIR RELATIONSHIP WITH SUPERVISOR

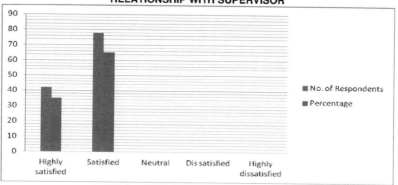

The above table and figure 4.6 depicts that 65% of the employees opined satisfied with working relationship with the superior and 35% of the employees opined that they are highly satisfied with the working relationship of the superior in the organization.

Hence it can be concluded that most of the employees are satisfied with the working relationship of the superior in the organization.

OPINION OF THE EMPLOYEES WITH REGARD TO RELATIONSHIP WITH THE CO-WORKER

TABLE - 4.7

OPINION OF EMPLOYEES ON SATISFACTION AND CO-WORKER RELATIONSHIP

Opinions	No. of Respondents	Percentage
Highly Satisfied	49	41
Satisfied	71	59
Neutral	0	0
Dissatisfied	0	0
Total	**120**	**100**

FIGURE - 4.7

GRAPHICAL REPRESENTATION OF THE OPINION OF EMPLOYEES ON SATISFACTION AND CO-WORKER RELATIONSHIP

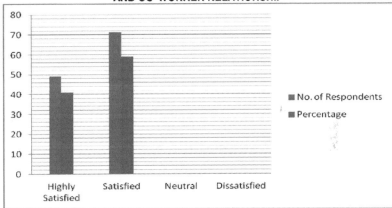

The above table and figure 4.7 depicts that 59% of the employees opined satisfied with working relationship with the co-worker and 41% of the employees opined that they are highly satisfied with the working relationship of the co-worker in the organization.

Hence it can be concluded that most of the employees are satisfied with the working relationship of the co-worker in the organization.

OPINION OF EMPLOYEES TOWARDS GRIEVANCE HANDLING PROCEDURE

TABLE - 4.8

EMPLOYEES OPINION ON SATISFACTION TOWARDS GRIEVANCE HANDLING PROCEDURE

Opinions	No. of Respondents	Percentage
Highly satisfied	9	8
Satisfied	111	92
Neutral	0	0
Dissatisfied	0	0
Total	120	100

FIGURE - 4.8

GRAPHICAL REPRESENTATION OF EMPLOYEES OPINION ON SATISFACTION TOWARDS GRIEVANCE HANDLING PROCEDURE

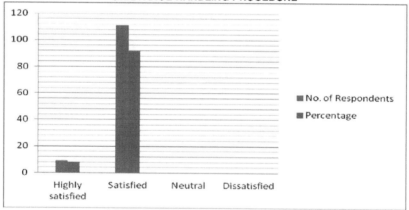

The above table and figure 4.8 depicts that 92% of the employees opined satisfied towards grievance handling procedure and 8% of the employees opined that they are highly satisfied towards grievance handling procedure in the organization.

Hence it can be concluded that most of the employees are satisfied towards grievance handling procedure in the organization.

OPINION OF EMPLOYEES WITH REGARD TO JOB SATISFACTION

TABLE - 4.9

EMPLOYEES OPINION ON JOB SATISFACTION

Opinions	No. of Respondents	Percentage
Highly satisfied	27	23
Satisfied	93	77
Neutral	0	0
Dissatisfied	0	0
Total	120	100

FIGURE - 4.9

GRAPHICAL REPRESENTATION OF EMPLOYEES OPINION ON JOB SATISFACTION

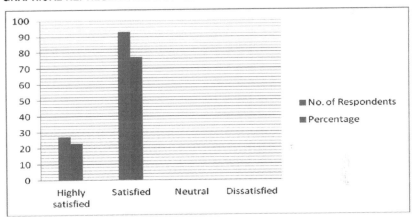

The above table and figure 4.9 depicts that 77% of the employees opined satisfied with their job and 23% of the employees opined that they are highly satisfied with their job in the organization.

Hence it can be concluded that most of the employees are satisfied with their job in the organization.

OPINION OF EMPLOYEES WITH REGARD TO THE BAD WORKING CONDITIONS IN THE ORGANIZATION

TABLE - 4.10
EMPLOYEES OPINION ON BAD WORKING CONDITIONS RESULTING IN ABSENTEEISM

Opinions	No. of Respondents	Percentage
Yes	0	0
No	87	72
Some times	33	28
Total	120	100

FIGURE - 4.10
GRAPHICAL REPRESENTATION OF EMPLOYEES OPINION ON BAD WORKING CONDITIONS RESULTING IN ABSENTEEISM

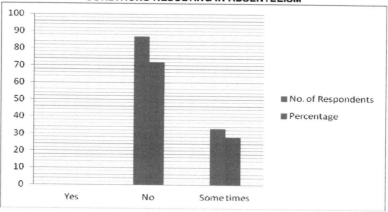

The above table and figure 4.10 depicts that 72% of the employees opined that there are no bad working conditions in the organization and 28% of the employees opined that sometimes they have been working in bad working conditions in the organization.

Hence it can be concluded that most of the employees expressed that there are no bad working conditions in the organization.

OPINION OF THE EMPLOYEES ON ABSENCE FROM DUTY BECAUSE OF HEAVY WORK LOAD

TABLE - 4.11

EMPLOYEES OPINION ON HEAVY WORK LOAD CAUSING ABSENTEEISM

Opinions	No. of Respondents	Percentage
Often	0	0
Rarely	49	42
Sometimes	1	0
Never	70	58
Total	120	100

FIGURE - 4.11

GRAPHICAL REPRESENTATION OF   EMPLOYEES OPINION ON HEAVY WORK LOAD
CAUSING ABSENTEEISM

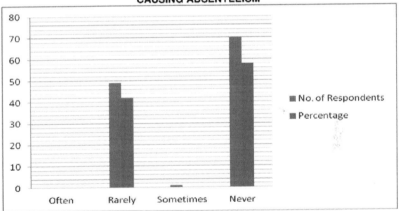

The above table and figure 4.11 depicts that 58% of the employees opined that they were never absent because of heavy work load and 42% of the employees opined that they were rarely absent because of the work load in the organization.

Hence it can be concluded that most of the employees opined that they were never absent because of heavy work load.

OPINION OF EMPLOYEES WITH REGARD TO SAFETY MEASURES PROVIDED BY THE ORGANIZATION

TABLE - 4.12
EMPLOYEES OPINION ON SAFETY MEASURES PROVIDED BY THE ORGANIZATION

Opinions	No. of Respondents	Percentage
Strongly agree	36	30
Agree	84	70
Neutral	0	0
Disagree	0	0
Strongly disagree	0	0
Total	**120**	**100**

FIGURE - 4.12
GRAPHICAL REPRESENTATION OF EMPLOYEES OPINION ON SAFETY MEASURES PROVIDED BY THE ORGANIZATION

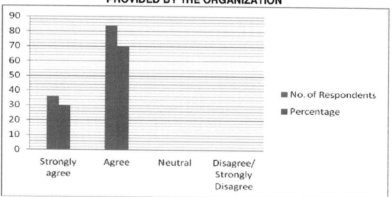

The above table and figure 4.12 depicts that 70% of the employees agreed to the safety measures that are provided by the organization and 30% of the employees agreed to the safety measures that are provided by the organization.

Hence it can be concluded that most of the employees of the employees agreed to the safety measures that are provided by the organization.

EMPLOYEES' OPINION REGARDING TO OTHER SOURCES OF INCOME

TABLE - 4.13

EMPLOYEES OPINION ON OTHER SOURCES OF INCOME

Opinions	No. of Respondents	Percentage
Agriculture	15	13
Business	0	0
Nothing	105	87
Total	120	100

FIGURE - 4.13

GRAPHICAL REPRESENTATION OF EMPLOYEES OPINION ON OTHER SOURCES OF INCOME

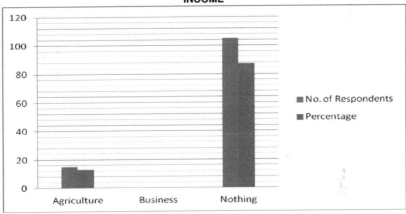

The above table and figure 4.13 depicts that 87% of the employees opined that they have got no other source of income and 13% of the employees have agreed that they have got agriculture and cultivating as other source of income.

Hence it can be concluded that most of the employees have go no other source of income.

OPINION OF EMPLOYEES ON THE ALLOTMENT OF SHIFT DUTY BY THE MANAGEMENT

TABLE - 4.14

EMPLOYEES OPINION ON SHIFT ALLOTMENT DUTY BY THE MANAGEMENT

Opinions	No. of Respondents	Percentage
1st shift	0	0
2nd shift	0	0
3rdshift	120	100
General shift	0	0
Total	120	100

FIGURE - 4.14

GRAPHICAL REPRESENTATION OF EMPLOYEES OPINION ON SHIFT ALLOTMENT DUTY BY THE MANAGEMENT

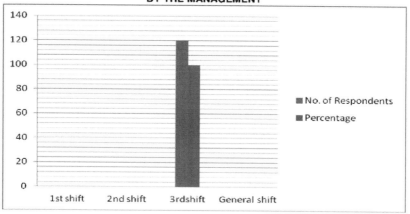

The above table and figure 4.14 depicts that 100% of the employees opined that they are comfortable with 2nd shift in the organization.

Hence it can be concluded that all the employees have expressed 2nd shift as the most convenient shift in the organization.

OPINION OF EMPLOYEES WITH REGARD TO THE NUMBER OF WORKING MEMBERS IN THE FAMILY

TABLE - 4.15

EMPLOYEES OPINION ON NUMBER OF WORKING MEMBERS IN THE FAMILY

Opinions	No. of Respondents	Percentage
One	86	71
Two	34	29
Above two	0	0
Total	120	100

FIGURE - 4.15

GRAPHICAL REPRESENTATION OF EMPLOYEES OPINION ON NUMBER OF WORKING MEMBERS IN THE FAMILY

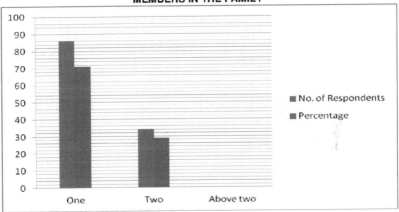

The above table and figure 4.15 depicts that 71% of the employees said that they have got another family member working elsewhere and 29% of the employees said that they have two members in the family working elsewhere.

Hence it can be concluded that most of the employees have another family member working elsewhere.

- 89 -

OPINION OF EMPLOYEES ON ABSENCE FROM DUTY BECAUSE OF REACHING FACTORY LATE

TABLE - 4.16

EMPLOYEES OPINION ON REACHING FACTORY LATE RESULTING TO ABSENTEEISM

Opinions	No. of Respondents	Percentage
Rarely	94	78
Sometimes	10	9
Always	0	0
Never	16	13
Total	120	100

FIGURE - 4.16

GRAPHICAL REPRESENTATION OF EMPLOYEES OPINION ON REACHING FACTORY LATE RESULTING TO ABSENTEEISM

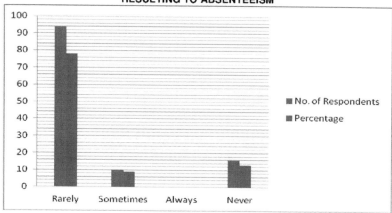

The above table and figure 4.16 depicts that 78% of the employees opined that they have got no other source of income and 13% of the employees have agreed that they have got agriculture and cultivating as other source of income.

Hence it can be concluded that most of the employees have go no other source of income.

- 90 -

OPINION OF EMPLOYEES ON THE SOURCE OF TRANSPORT CHOOSEN FOR ARRIVAL TO THE FACTORY

TABLE - 4.17
EMPLOYEES OPINION REGARDING ARRIVAL TO THE FACTORY

Opinions	No. of Respondents	Percentage
By bus	33	27
By bicycle	8	8
By scooter	79	65
On foot	0	0
Total	120	100

FIGURE - 4.17
GRAPHICAL REPRESENTATION OF EMPLOYEES OPINION REGARDING ARRIVAL TO THE FACTORY

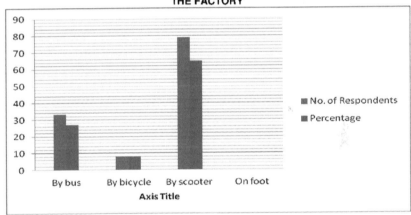

The above table and figure 4.17 depicts that 65% of the employees opined that they have two-wheeler as a source to arrive at the factory, 27% of the employees' opined bus as a source of transport and 8% bicycle as a source to arrive at the factory.

Hence it can be concluded that most of the employees have two-wheeler as a source of transport to arrive at the factory premises.

OPINION OF EMPLOYEES WITH REGARD TO THE BAD HABITS

TABLE - 4.18

EMPLOYEES OPINION ON THEIR BAD HABITS CAUSING ABSENTEEISM

Opinions	No. of Respondents	Percentage
Alcohol	0	0
Smoking	0	0
Gambling	0	0
Nothing	120	100
Total	120	100

FIGURE - 4.18

GRAPHICAL REPRESENTATION OF EMPLOYEES OPINION ON THEIR BAD HABITS CAUSING ABSENTEEISM

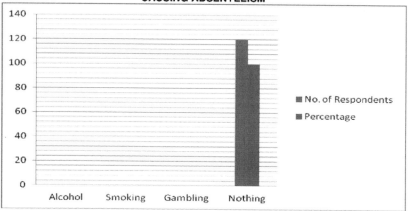

The above table and figure 4.18 depicts that 100% of the employees have opined that they are not addicted of any type of bad habits such as alcohol, smoking and gambling.

Hence it can be concluded that most of the employees have bad habits such as alcohol, smoking and gambling.

OPINION OF EMPLOYEES ON EXTRA HEALTH AND HYGIENIC BENEFITS THAT ARE TO BE PROVIDED BY THE ORGANISATION

TABLE - 4.19

EMPLOYEES OPINION ON THE EXTRA HEALTH AND HYGIENIC BENEFITS

Opinions	No. of Respondents	Percentage
Yes	8	7
No	97	80
Neutral	15	13
Total	120	100

FIGURE - 4.19

GRAPHICAL REPRESENTATION OF EMPLOYEES OPINION ON THE EXTRA HEALTH AND HYGIENIC BENEFITS

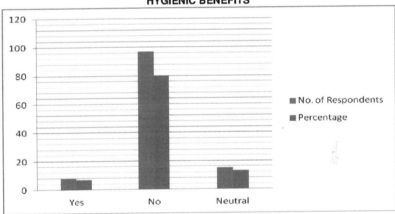

The above table and figure 4.19 depicts that 80% of the employees opined that no extra and hygienic benefits are being provided by the organization, 13% opined neutral, and 7% opined that the employees are provided extra and hygienic benefits are being provided by the organization

Hence it can be concluded that most of the employees have no extra and hygienic benefits are being provided by the organization.

OPINION OF EMPLOYEES WITH REGARD TO THE HEALTH PROBLEMS

TABLE - 4.20

EMPLOYEES OPINION ON HEALTH PROBLEMS LEADING TO ABSENTEEISM

Opinions	No. of Respondents	Percentage
Yes	9	8
No	111	92
Neutral	0	0
Total	120	100

FIGURE - 4.20

GRAPHICAL REPRESENTATION OF the EMPLOYEES OPINION ON HEALTH PROBLEMS LEADING TO ABSENTEEISM

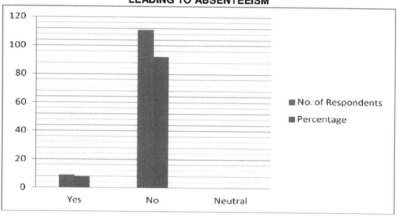

The above table and figure 4.20 depicts that 92% of the employees opined that they have got no health problems and 8% of the employees opined that they have got some health problem.

Hence it can be concluded that most of the employees have got no health problem.

OPINION OF EMPLOYEES ON WELFARE FACILITIES PROVIDED BY THE ORGANIZATION

TABLE - 4.21

OPINION OF EMPLOYEES ON THE WELFARE FACILITIES PROVIDED BY THE ORGANIZATION

Opinions	No. of Respondents	Percentage
Highly satisfied	34	29
Satisfied	86	71
Dissatisfied	0	0
Highly dissatisfied	0	0
Total	120	100

FIGURE - 4.21

GRAPHICAL REPRESENTATION OF THE OPINION OF EMPLOYEES ON THE WELFARE FACILITIES PROVIDED BY THE ORGANIZATION

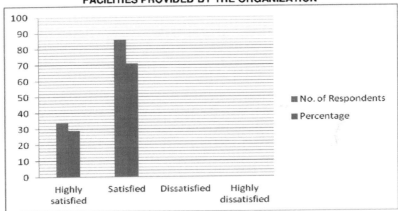

The above table and figure 4.21 depicts that 71% of the employees opined that are satisfied with the welfare facilities and 29% of the employees felt highly satisfied with the welfare facilities that are provided by the organization.

Hence it can be concluded that most of the employees opined satisfied with the welfare facilities provided by the organization.

THERE IS NO SIGNIFICANT DIFFERENCE BETWEEN SUPERIOR AND SUBORDINATE EMPLOYEES WITH REGARD TO ABSENTEEISM IN RMM FOOD PRODUCTS PRIVATE LIMITED

TABLE NO. 4.22

EMPLOYEES OPINION ON ABSENTEEISM WITH REGARD TO DESIGNATION

S.NO	Variables	No. of Respondents	Mean (SD)	Mean Difference @ 95% CI	p-value p<0.0001
1	Superior	30	61.97 (4.86)	0.89	0.0048
2	Subordinate	90	59.69 (3.33)	0.35	

t test results

P value and statistical significance: The two-tailed P value equals to 0.0048

Confidence interval: The mean of Superior minus Subordinate equals 2.28; 95% confidence interval of this difference: From 0.71 to 3.85

Intermediate values used in calculations: $t = 2.8718$; $do = 118$ standard error of difference = 0.793

Table 4.22 shows that the by conventional criteria, this difference is considered to be very statistically significant.

Henceforth, it can be concluded that there is a lot of difference of opinion between superior and subordinated employees with regard to absenteeism

THERE IS NO SIGNIFICANT DIFFERENCE BETWEEN MALE AND FEMALE EMPLOYEES WITH REGARD TO ABSENTEEISM IN RMM FOOD PRODUCTS PRIVATE LIMITED

TABLE NO. 4.23

EMPLOYEES OPINION ON ABSENTEEISM WITH REGARD TO SEX

S.NO	Variables	No. of Respondents	Mean(SD)	Mean Difference @ 95% CI	p-value $p<0.0001$
1	Male	96	60.63 (3.33)	0.34	0.8136
2	Female	24	60.83 (5.56)	1.14	

t test results

P value and statistical significance: The two-tailed P value equals 0.8136
Confidence interval: The mean of Male and Female equals 0.21,   95% confidence interval of this difference: From -1.95 to 1.54
Intermediate values used in calculations: t = 0.2362;   df = 118; standard error of difference = 0.882

Table 4.23 shows that   by conventional criteria, this difference is considered to be not statistically significant.

Henceforth, it can be concluded that there is no significant difference of opinion between male and female employees regard to absenteeism

THERE IS NO SIGNIFICANT DIFFERENCE BETWEEN BELOW 40 YEARS AND ABOVE 40 YEARS OF AGE EMPLOYEES WITH REGARD TO QUALITY OF WORK LIFE IN SRINALA LEATHERS PVIVATE LIMITED

TABLE NO. 4.24

EMPLOYEES OPINION ON ABSENTEEISM WITH REGARD TO AGE

S.NO	Variables	No. of Respondents	Mean(SD)	Mean Difference @ 95% CI	p-value p<0.0001
1	Below 40	75	60.51 (3.83)	0.44	0.6444
2	Above 40	45	60.84 (3.95)	0.59	

t test results

P value and statistical significance: The two-tailed P value equals 0.6444

Confidence interval: The mean of Below 40 minus Above 40 equals -0.34, 95% confidence interval of this difference: From -1.78 to 1.11

Intermediate values used in calculations: $t = 0.4627$; $df = 118$; standard error of difference = 0.730

Table 4. 24 show that by conventional criteria, this difference is considered to be not statistically significant.

Henceforth, it can be concluded that there is no significant difference of opinion between below 40 and above 40 years of age employees regard to absenteeism

THERE IS NO SIGNIFICANT DIFFERENCE BETWEEN DEGREE/DIPLOMA AND PG/PROFESSIONAL QULIFICATION EMPLOYEES WITH REGARD TO QUALITY OF WORK LIFE IN SRINALA LEATHERS PVIVATE LIMITED

TABLE NO. 4.25

EMPLOYEES OPINION ON ABSENTEEISM WITH REGARD TO QUALIFICATION

S.NO	Variables	No. of Respondents	Mean (SD)	Mean Difference @ 95% CI	p-value p<0.0001
1	Degree/ Diploma	113	60.35 (3.43)	0.32	0.0006
2	PG/ Professional	7	65.43 (7.07)	2.67	

t test results

P value and statistical significance: The two-tailed P value is less than 0.0006

Confidence interval: The mean of Degree/Diploma minus PG/Professional Qualification equals -5.08; 95% confidence interval of this difference: From -7.94 to -2.23

Intermediate values used in calculations: t=3.5254; df=118; standard error of difference=1.442

Table 4.25 shows that by conventional criteria, this difference is considered to be extremely statistically significant.

Henceforth, it can be concluded that there is extremely significant difference of opinion between degree/diploma and PG/Professional employees regard to absenteeism

THERE IS NO SIGNIFICANT DIFFERENCE BETWEEN 0-10 AND 10-20 YEARS OF SERVICE OF EMPLOYEES WITH REGARD TO ABSENTEEISM IN RMM FOOD PRODUCTS PRIVATE LIMITED

TABLE NO. 4.26

EMPLOYEES OPINION ON ABSENTEEISM WITH REGARD TO SERVICE

S.NO	Variables	No. of Respondents	Mean (SD)	Mean Difference @ 95% CI	p-value p<0.0001
1	0-10	75	60.43 (3.97)	0.46	0.3961
2	10-20	45	61.04 (3.63)	0.54	

t test results

P value and statistical significance: The two-tailed P value equals 0.3961,

Confidence interval: The mean of Male minus Female equals -0.62; 95% confidence interval of this difference: From -2.05 to 0.82

Intermediate values used in calculations: t=0.8517; df=118; standard error of difference=0.725

Table 4.26 shows that by conventional criteria, this difference is considered to be not statistically significant.

Henceforth, it can be concluded that there is no significant difference of opinion between 0-10 years and 10-20 years of service employees regard to absenteeism

FINDINGS

1. 80% of the employees opined that they are rarely absent because of unexpected work.

2. 74% of the employees opined that they are rarely absent because of health reasons.

3. 96% of the employees opined that they never take leave without permission.

4. 85% of the employees opined satisfied with the compensation paid for the work they perform.

5. 66% of the employees opined satisfied with the working environment provided by the organization.

6. 65% of the employees opined satisfied with working relationship with the superior.

7. 59% of the employees opined satisfied with working relationship with the co-worker.

8. 92% of the employees opined satisfied towards grievance handling procedure.

9. 77% of the employees opined satisfied with their job.

10. 72% of the employees opined that there are no bad working conditions in the organization.

11. 58% of the employees opined that they were never absent because of heavy work load.

12. 70% of the employees agreed to the safety measures that are provided by the organization.

13. 87% of the employees opined that they have got no other source of income.

14. 100% of the employees opined that they are comfortable with 2nd shift in the organization.

15. 71% of the employees said that they have got another family member working elsewhere.

16. 78% of the employees opined that they have got no other source of income.

17. 65% of the employees opined that they have got two wheeler as a source to arrive at the factory.

18. 100% of the employees have opined that they are not addicted of any type of bad habits such as alcohol, smoking and gambling.

19. 80% of the employees opined that no extra and hygienic benefits are being provided by the organization.

20. 92% of the employees opined that they have got no health problems.

21. 71% of the employees opined that are satisfied with the welfare facilities that are provided by the organization.

22. There is a lot of difference of opinion between superior and subordinate employees with regard to absenteeism.

23. There is no significant difference of opinion between male and female employees regard to absenteeism

24. There is no significant difference of opinion between below 40 and above 40 years of age employees regard to absenteeism

25. There is extremely significant difference of opinion between degree/diploma and PG/Professional employees regard to absenteeism

26.   there is no significant difference of opinion between 0-10 years and 10-20 years of service employees   regard to absenteeism

SUGGESTIONS

The effect of absenteeism firstly reduces the income of the workmen on the principle of "No work No Pay". Consequently the loss is also to the employer both in discipline and efficiency and thus the organization suffers due to loss of production and income.

The absenteeism affects adversely both the employee and the worker and give rise to many industrial unrest and labor problem. It also affects the attitude of the workers towards industry and industrial life.

Important measures that have to be taken by the management are as follows:

- Encouraging good attendance through incentives schemes.
- Award linked with attendance.
- Counseling.
- Social and Psychological counseling.
- HRD Programmes
- Through circulars.
- Review of absenteeism
- Guidelines for punishments
- Motivating the employees
- Conducting workshops.
- Monthly analysis of absenteeism
- Adoption of chronic absenteeism by executives.

CONCLUSION

It has been found that there is a significant difference of opinions between superior and subordinate employees with regard to the factors that lead to absenteeism. There seems to be an extremely significant difference between degree/diploma and pg/post-graduation employees with regard to absenteeism. The overall study with regard to absenteeism indicates that there is low absenteeism in the organization and the organization seems to be successful in adopting the measures to reduce employee absenteeism

1. Mirza saiyadin (1988), Tata Mc GrawHill Publications, 3rd edition, New Delhi.

2. Wayne F. Cascio (1986), Tata Mc Graw Hill Publications, 6th Edition, New Delhi.

3. David B .Balkin (2001) , Prentice-Hall Pvt., Ltd., 3rd Edition, New Delhi.

4. George Bohalander and Vienna Vera (2010),1st Edition, Engage Learning India Pvt., Ltd, Australia.

5. V.K Sharma (2002), VIVA Books Pvt., Ltd., New Delhi, Mumbai.

6. Gupta (1996), Sultan Chand and sons, 9th edition, New Delhi.

7. Rakish k. Choprav (1989), First and Second edition, Kitab Mahal, Allahabad, pp.380-381.

8. Ushers,(2010), Journal of Business Management, Christ university.

9. L.M. Prasad (2007), Sultan Chand & Sons, 2nd Edition, New Delhi.

10. V.K Sharma (2002), VIVA books Pvt., Ltd., New Delhi.

11. Berman, Peter, and Dexter Cuizon. 2004. Multiple public-private jobholding of health care providers in developing countries: An exploration of theory and evidence. London, UK: DFID Health Systems Resource Centre. http://collections.europarchive.org/tna/20100918075 642/http://www.dfidhealthrc.org/publications/health   service_delivery/ Berman Cuizon.pdf (accessed February 7, 2012).

12. The Capacity Project. 2009. "What about the health workers?" Improving the work climate at rural facilities in Kenya. Voices from the Capacity Project, no. 27. Chapel Hill, NC: The Capacity Project. http://www.capacityproject.org/images/stories/Voices/voices_27.pdf(acc essed March 15, 2012).

13. Chaudhury, Nazmul, and Jeffrey S. Hammer. 2003. Ghost doctors: Absenteeism in Bangladeshi health facilities. Policy Research Working Paper 3065. Washington, DC: The World Bank. http://www-wds.worldbank.org/external/default/WDSContentServer/IW3P/IB/2003/0 7/22/000094946_03070804210190/Rendered/PDF/multi0page.pdf (accessed February 8, 2012).

14. Chaudhury, Nazmul, Jeffrey Hammer, Michael Kremer, Karthik Muralidharan, and F. Halsey Rogers. 2006. "Missing in action: Teacher and health worker absence in developing countries." Journal of Economic Perspectives 20(1):91-116.

15. Dobalen, Andrew, and Waly Wane. 2008. Informal payments and moonlighting in Tajikistan's health sector. Policy Research Working Paper 4555. Washington, DC: The World Bank. http://papers.ssrn.com/sol3/ papers .cfm ? abstract _id=1106044 (accessed February 8, 2012).

16. Doerr, Rick. 2012. Utilizing mobile money in healthcare. ICT4Development: Global Broadband and Innovations. Washington, DC: USAID. http://gbiportal.net/2012/01/27/utilizing-mobile-money-in-healthcare/ (accessed March 15, 2012).

17. Hilhorst, T., D. Bagayoko, D. Dao, E. Lodenstein, and J. Toonen. 2005. Building effective local partnerships for improved basic social services delivery in Mali. Amsterdam, the Netherlands: Royal Tropical Institute (KIT) and Bamako, Mali: SNV. http://www. kit. nl/ net /KIT _ Publicaties _output/ShowFile2.aspx?e=871 (accessed March 15, 2012).

18. Hsiao, William C., and Peter S. Heller. 2007. What macroeconomists should know about health care policy. Washington, DC: International Monetary Fund. http://apin.harvard.edu/health-care-financing /files / hsiao_2007_what_macroeconomists_should_know_about_health_polic y.pdf (accessed March 6, 2012).

19. Kiwanuka, Suzanne N., Alison A. Kinengyere, Christine Nalwadda, Freddie Ssengooba, Olico Okui, and George W. Pariyo. 2010. Effects of interventions to manage dual practice (protocol). Cochrane Database of Systematic Reviews 3. http://www.who.int/alliance-hpsr / projects / alliancehpsr_sruganda_kiwanuka.pdf (accessed February 7, 2012).

20. Institute of Policy Analysis and Research (IPAR). 2008. Absenteeism of health care providers in Machakos District, Kenya. IPAR Policy Brief 12, no. 2. http://www.docstoc.com/docs/69200071/Absenteeism-of-Health-Care-Providers-in-Machakos-District--Kenya (accessed February 8, 2012).

21. Lewis, Maureen, and Gunilla Pettersson. 2009. Governance in health care delivery: Raising performance. Policy Research Working Paper 5074. Washington, DC: The World Bank. http://www-wds.worldbank.org/external/default/WDSContentServer/IW3P/IB/2009/1

0/13/000158349_20091013151915/Rendered/PDF/WPS5074.pdf(acce
ssed February 7, 2012).

22. Macq, Jean, Paulo Ferrinho, Vincent De Brouwere, and Wim Van Lerberghe. 2001. "Managing health services in developing countries: Between the ethics of the civil servant and the need for moonlighting: Managing and moonlighting." Human Resources for Health Development Journal (HRDJ) 5, no. 1-3. http://www.who.int/hrh/en/HRDJ_5_03.pdf (accessed February 8, 2012).

23. Matsiko, Charles Wycliffe. 2011. Absenteeism in Uganda: Quantifying the nature and extent of absenteeism rates at the district level. Kampala, Uganda: IntraHealth International.

24. Meessen, Bruno, Laurent Musango, Jean-Pierre I. Kashala, and Jackie Lemlin. 2006. Reviewing institutions of rural health centres: The Performance Initiative in Butare, Rwanda. Tropical Medicine and International Health 11(8):1303–1317.

25. http://onlinelibrary.wiley.com/doi/10.1111/j.1365-156.2006.01680.x/full (accessed March 20, 2012); and Dieleman, Marjolein, and Jan Willem Harnmeijer. 2006. Improving health worker performance: In search of promising practices. Geneva, Switzerland: World Health Organization.

26. http://www.who.int/hrh/resources/improving_hw_performance.pdf (accessed March 20, 2012).

27. National Commission on Macroeconomics and Health (NCMH). 2005. Financing and delivery of health care services in India. NCMH Background Paper. New Delhi, India: National Commission on Macroeconomics and Health, Ministry of Health and Family Welfare. http://www.who.int/macrohealth/action/Background%20Papers%20repo rt.pdf (accessed March 6, 2012).

28. Vujicic, Marko. 2010. The public private mix. Presentation at HRH Labor Markets Training Course; August 12, 2010. http: // www . ghwen . org / app/controllers/training/hrh/D2_b_PublicPrivate_Vujicic.ppt (accessed February 7, 2012).

29. Vujicic, Marko, Kelechi Ohiri, and Susan Sparkes. 2009. Working in health: Financing and managing the public sector health workforce. Washington DC: The World Bank. http:// www . who . int /

workforcealliance/knowledge/publications/partner/workinginhealth_vujici
c_worldbank_2009.pdf (accessed March 7, 2012)

30. World Health Organization (WHO). 2006. The world health report 2006: Working together for health. Geneva, Switzerland: World Health Organization. http://www.who.int/whr/2006/en/ (accessed February 8, 2012).

Questionnaire on Employee Absenteeism

Designation   :
Age   : Below 40/Above 40
Gender   : Male/Female
Qualification   : Diploma/ Degree ,PG/ Professional
Experience   : 0-10 years , 10-20 years, 20& above

SERIOUS ACCIDENTS

1. You are absent because you have unexpected work?
   a. Rarely b. Sometimes   c. Always   d. Never

2 .Health is one reason you are absent to the duty?
   a. Rarely   b. Sometimes   c. Always   d. Never

LOW MORALE

3. How often do you take leave without giving information?
   a. Always   b. Never   c. Sometimes

4. What is your opinion regarding the pay?
   a. Highly satisfied b. satisfied   c. dissatisfied   d. Highly dissatisfied

5 .Are you satisfied working in your organization?
   a. Highly satisfied b. satisfied   c. Dissatisfied   d. Highly dissatisfied

6. How do you feel about the relationship with supervisor?
   a. Highly satisfied   b. satisfied   c. Dissatisfied   d. Highly dissatisfied

7. What is your opinion about relationship with co-worker?
   a. Highly Satisfied   b. Satisfied   c. Natural   d. Dissatisfied

BOREDOM OF THE JOB

8. Are you satisfied towards grievance handling procedure?
   a. Highly Satisfied   b. Satisfied   c. Netural   d. Dissatisfied

9. What is your opinion regarding the satisfaction of job?
   a. Highly satisfied   b. Satisfied   c. Netural   d. Dissatisfied

POOR WORKING CONDITION

10. Do you absent because of bad conditions ?
    a. Yes   b. No   c. Sometimes

11. Do you absent because of heavy workload?

    a. Often   b. Rarely c. Sometimes   d. Never

12. You are Satisfied with the safety measures provided by the Management . Do you agree?

    a. Strongly agree b. Agree   c. Disagree   d. strongly disagree

13. Do you have any other sources of income like?

    a. Agriculture b. Business   C. Nothing

14. In which shift you are facing more problems to attend the duty?

    a. 1st shift   b.2nd shift   c.3rd shift   d. General Shift

15. Number of working members in the family ?

    a. One   b. Two   c. Above two

TRANASPORATION PROBLEM

16.You are absent because of your reaching factory late?

    a .Rarely   b. Sometimes   c. Always   d. Never

17. How do you come to the factory ?

    a. By Bus   b. By Bicycle c. By Scooter   d. On foot

STRESS

18. Did you addict to any bad habit like ?

    a. Alcohol   b. Smoking   c .Gambling   d. Nothing

19. Whether you need any extra health and hygienic benefits?

    a. Yes   b. No   c. Neutral

20. Are you facing health problems often ?

    a . Yes   b. No   c. Neutral

POOR WELFARE FACILITIES

21. What is your opinion regarding welfare facilities ?

    a. Highly satisfied b. Satisfied c. Dissatisfied d. Highly Dissatisfied

Druck: KN Digital Printforce GmbH · Schockenriedstraße 37 · 70565 Stuttgart